Best *of* Breed

THE **BOXER**

Your Essential Guide
From Puppy To
Senior Dog

Edited By
Viv Matthews

ACKNOWLEDGEMENTS
The publishers would like to acknowledge the following for help with photography: Viv Matthews (Brubor), Marion Seeney (Maranseen), Laura Clark (Clarkenwells), Sue Harvey (Faerdorn), Sue Drinkwater (Sulez), Walker and Yvonne Miller (Walkon), Gillian Thompson (with Henry) and Carolyne Lewis.

Cover photo: © Tracy Morgan Animal Photography (www.animalphotographer.co.uk)
page 9 © istockphoto.com/Greg Nicholas; page 11 © istockphoto.com/Karen Givens
page 15 © istockphoto.com/ene; page 18 © istockphoto.com/Lynette Judd
page 36 © istockphoto.com/Emmanuelle Bonzami; page 38 © istockphoto.com/Justin Horrocks;
page 39 © istockphoto.com/Tanya Lug; page 41 © istockphoto.com/Greg Nicholas;
page 45 © istockphoto.com/Serdar Yaga; page 62 © istockphoto.com/Leisa Hennessy;
page 68 © istockphoto.com/Denisa Moorehouse; page 87 © istockphoto.com/Robert Weber;
page 88 © istockphoto.com/Michelle Harvey; page 110 © istockphoto.com/Iztoc Noc;
page 120 © istockphoto.com/Alan Hess; page 133 © istockphoto.com/Ludovic Rhodes

The British Breed Standard reproduced in Chapter 7 is the copyright of the Kennel Club and published with the club's kind permission. Extracts from the American Breed Standard are reproduced by kind permission of the American Kennel Club.

THE QUESTION OF GENDER
**The 'he' pronoun is used throughout this book in favour of the rather impersonal 'it',
but no gender bias is intended.**

First published in 2008 by the Pet Book Publishing Company Limited
St Martin's Farm, Chapel Lane, Zeals, Wiltshire BA12 6NZ.

This edition first published in 2015
© 2008 and 2010 Pet Book Publishing Company Limited.
Printed and bound in South Korea.

ISBN
978-1-910488-13-3
1-910488-13-5

CONTENTS

GETTING TO KNOW BOXERS

Chapter 1

It has often been said that once you have had a Boxer then you will always have a Boxer, as all other breeds pale into insignificance against this fun-loving, energetic family dog. This statement is certainly true for the many people who have never looked back once a Boxer has become a member of their family. Why should this be? Is it the Boxer's appearance, with his gleaming short coat, the lovely clean lines, athletic, muscular build and a unique blocky head with expressive dark eyes that mirror your soul? Or is it the Boxer's great character, so tactile and protective of his family yet never treacherous, even in old age?

When a Boxer joins your family it is like having another child, as a Boxer does not realise that he is a canine and wants to do everything that you do… and I mean everything! A Boxer likes to get up

close; it is one of the most tactile breeds that I know. They are not for the faint-hearted! For me, no other breed even comes close to this over-the-top, fun-loving, boisterous, 'in your face' dog!

I grew up in the country in a house that was also home to an endless procession of pet animals, which always included a couple of dogs of dubious parentage. My father was often heard to say, "You can't beat a good mongrel. They are much better than any of those pedigree dogs. All pedigree dogs are inbred." But that was before he met Carlo!

When I was 13 years old, I answered an advertisement for a dog walker to exercise a Boxer called Carlo while his family was out at work. For the princely sum of £1 a week, I walked him twice a day and grew to love him. During the school holidays, his walks lasted all day, as I couldn't

bear to leave him on his own in his kennel. Six months later, his owners said they were moving and they would have to find him a home or have him put down. Despite the fact that we already had a large, brown, shaggy mongrel and three cats, I begged my father to let me have Carlo. He came to live with us and was adored by all the family. Eventually, when I got married, Carlo stayed with my parents, as he was elderly. When the time came to say goodbye to him, my parents begged me to help them get another Boxer, because the house was so empty without him. So much for: "You can't beat a good mongrel!"

PHYSICAL CHARACTERISTICS

The Boxer is a medium-sized, square dog of good substance, with clean lines and powerful muscles under a short, glossy coat. The colours permitted under the Breed Standard, which is the blueprint describing the ideal Boxer, are brindle and fawn. Brindle consists of black stripes on a fawn or red background, the dark stripes varying from heavy to sparse. The fawn colour can range from a very pale gold, right through to a dark deer red. There may or may not be white markings, which, if present, should not exceed more than a third of the background colour. White markings, if present, are usually confined to the feet and legs, chest and a flash or blaze of white on the head.

A fully-grown Boxer is a thing of beauty to look at with his flowing lines and solid bone, combining substance with elegance. His head is what gives the unique stamp to the breed, having a broad, blunt muzzle with an undershot jaw, and a chin that can be viewed from all sides. His expression is always alert, and dark, intelligent eyes show great love and trust.

An adult male Boxer stands between 22.5 inches and 25 inches (57-63 cms) at the shoulder, weighing 30-32 kgs (66-70 lbs). Bitches tend to be slightly smaller, being between 21-23 inches at the shoulder (53-59 cms) and weighing 25-27 kgs, (55-60 lbs).

The Boxer is a dog of substance, built on clean muscular lines.

WHITE BOXERS

It has to be remembered that while the breed was being developed, many of its ancestors were predominantly white or parti-colours, and this remained so for many years.

During the First World War, when Boxers were deployed in the armed services, it became obvious that white dogs were not the ideal choice for guard or patrol dogs, as they could be seen in the dark. Solid brindles and fawns were the obvious choice, and many Boxers served their country well during the war years. But as a result, it was decided that white Boxers no longer conformed to the Breed Standard and were therefore not eligible for competition in the show ring.

Today, when selecting a dog for the show ring, it is fashionable to have smart white markings on the head and feet; that is to say, a neat white blaze and even white socks, which attract the eye rather like a white handkerchief in the breast pocket of a dark suit. But it is stipulated in the Breed Standard that white markings should not exceed one-third of the background colour.

Thus, if we mate a flashy dog to a bitch that is similarly marked, both will carry the gene for white, and, as an average guide, 25 per cent of the resulting puppies will be white. In a litter of eight, two pups will possibly be white, with or without coloured patches. But as Mother Nature can be diverse, some litters will have no white at

As a result of the breed's ancestry, white puppies occur regularly in Boxer litters.

all, and some may have more than 25 per cent of white coloured puppies.

White is not a colour that is recognised by the Breed Standard, and these puppies cannot be registered or bred from. However, they are often seen competing at the highest level in the obedience and agility rings. I usually recommend that white Boxers are neutered to avoid mismatings.

Most breeders will sell their white puppies much more cheaply than their coloured littermates, usually at least half the price. Beware any

unscrupulous breeder that claims their white puppies are 'rare', and therefore command a much higher price. They are nothing of the sort.

Some breeders will have their white puppies destroyed at birth due to the fact that, in common with many white animals, they can carry the gene for deafness and may be deaf. It is said that if a white Boxer has a coloured patch, he will not be deaf, but I have sold many pure white hearing dogs in the 30 years that I have been breeding – in fact, I have only ever had two deaf puppies in this time.

LIVING WITH A DEAF DOG

A deaf dog needs a really special home with owners that have loads of time and patience, which is not easy to find these days where life seems to be lived in the fast lane! If you already have a hearing dog as a companion then this makes life a little easier.

A friend of mine, Gillian Thompson) came to see a litter that I had, as I was worried that one of the puppies was deaf. After some painstaking tests we decided that he was, but he kept making a beeline for Gillian and chewing her shoes. She fell in love with him, christened him Henry, and begged me to let her try to train him. She had three other Boxers, which helped enormously, as he tended to follow them, but he quickly learnt to recognise handsignals and read body language. Gillian took him to local training classes and he romped through the classes, even doing his bronze Good Citizen test, which he passed with flying colours. In 2006, Henry represented the breed at Crufts, competing in an obedience demonstration over two days, where he didn't put a paw wrong. When the media discovered that he was deaf, Gillian was interviewed on television, and the following day he proved very popular with the general public who wanted to see this amazing dog. Gillian said it was the proudest day of her life, but she also has to take the credit for the love, dedication and determination that have been vital elements in training a deaf dog.

SIGN LANGUAGE

Gillian Thompson has taught Henry basic obedience purely through sign language, as he is profoundly deaf.

1. **Henry responds to the Sit command.**
2. **He follows the handsignal and goes into a Down.**
3. **The thumbs-up sign which shows Henry he has done well!**

If you decide to buy a white puppy, ensure that his hearing has been checked by a vet to save any heartache later on.

BOXERS WITH TAILS

Boxers have always been customarily docked, however from 6 April 2007, the law changed and the docking of dogs' tails is now banned for cosmetic reasons, so all Boxers born in the United Kingdom, in line with many other countries, now have long tails.

Boxers have always been docked, and there is no doubt in my mind that a correctly docked tail adds that extra sharpness to an ultra-smart outline, thus completing the overall balance.

Originally the Boxer's tail was docked and the ears were cropped because it gave less

opportunity for an opponent to get a grip when dogs were fighting. In more modern times, tail docking has been carried out purely for cosmetic reasons.

In my experience as a breeder, puppies legally docked at around three days of age seem to feel very little pain, and this has been supported by medical evidence. Our own litters have been normally done in the presence of their dam and get straight back on to the milk bar and continue feeding straight afterwards.

There are some exemptions from the ban for certain working dogs and also for medical reasons. Puppies may be docked if evidence has been provided that they are likely to be working in Her Majesty's armed forces, emergency rescue, pest control, or when working as gundogs.

As far as the Boxer is concerned, long tails will mean a vast upheaval for the breed. It will completely alter the whole balance of the Boxer, and it will be interesting to see the variety of shapes and thicknesses of tails, since we have never had to breed for tail type! There will no doubt have to be a new clause in the Standard to take this into account.

It is too soon to tell whether the ban on tail docking will affect the popularity of the breed, or show entries. Some older breeders are unable to accept the new legislation and have stated that they will no longer continue to breed and show Boxers. To me, this seems a great shame. The Boxer is so much more than a short stumpy tail. I first fell in love with their great looks, it is

The breed was customarily docked, but we are now getting used to seeing Boxers with long tails.

true, but it is their amazing personality that has endeared me to the breed, and a long tail will never change that!

I do wonder about the Boxer's enthusiastic, boisterous nature, coupled with a furiously wagging rudder, which is quite likely to sweep ornaments from coffee tables and whip your legs black

and blue! We shall have to get used to moving valued possessions up that bit higher and stand well back from the wagging end.

Tail damage is also a likely possibility, and in Sweden where docking was banned over 10 years ago, veterinary reports claim that 17 per cent of Boxers

are damaging their long tails in and around their home environment. The damage ranges from splits to full breaks, often requiring amputation

It remains to be seen whether long tails will affect the popularity of the breed as a family dog. I do hope not.

BOBTAILS:
A NEW WAY FORWARD

We are fortunate within the breed to have an eminent breed geneticist, namely Dr Bruce Cattanach BSc, DSc, PhD who is owner of the Steynmere Boxers.

Bruce had contemplated the idea of breeding Boxers with short tails for over 20 years, when he decided to do a test cross of two screw-tailed Boxers. The mating was unsuccessful, as the resulting litter all had normal tails, showing that the screw tail is not inherited.

A more positive study, involving a cross to a bobtailed dog of a different breed and then backcrossing the descendants to Boxers, proved more successful. The results of the first two generations of the cross were reported in three 1996 issues of the weekly dog paper *Dog World*. A further report was published in August 1998 and described the third- and fourth-generation backcrosses, the last making them eligible for entry into the Kennel Club Boxer Registry.

Initially, a white Boxer bitch was mated to a Pembroke Welsh Corgi dog, which carried a single dose of the gene causing a bobtail. Then, through a series of backcrosses to Boxers in each subsequent generation, the bobtail gene was gradually established in a Boxer genetic background.

Steynmere Hot Shot, a fourth-generation male, with a bobtail, was shown with reasonable success for a solid dog, before going to Norway to be used at stud. Within a few months of his arrival, interest in the bobtail Boxer escalated enormously. Swedish and Dutch Boxer breeders also plan to use this dog, and his sperm has already gone for artificial insemination in Finland.

With the banning of docking in the UK, it remains to be seen whether there will be an upsurge in bobtails as an alternative to having a Boxer with a long tail.

THE ACTIVE BOXER

A Boxer needs a reasonable amount of free-running daily to take the tickle out of his toes, combined with a certain amount of lead exercise.

We aim to exercise our Boxers for half an hour twice daily, usually early in the morning and in the evening, thus avoiding the midday heat in summer. It is never a good idea to take a Boxer out when the weather is very hot, as, due to his boisterous nature, he never knows when he has had enough and could become overheated. The exercise we give usually takes the form of 20 minutes on the lead with a 10-minute blast off the lead.

A Boxer will happily join his owners on a 10-mile hike or equally enjoy a short lead walk. Do not just put your dog out in the garden in the hope that he will exercise himself; he will just wait at the door until you join him. In fact, a Boxer is miserable when he is shut out on his own and may resort to destructive

Breeders are now experimenting with producing Boxers with naturally short tails.

Steynmere If She will: Sired by Ch. Steynmere Just William out of a bobtail bitch, this Boxer won a number of Firsts at Championship shows and qualified for Crufts several times.

This is a lively and energetic breed that needs regular, varied exercise.

A THINKING DOG

First and foremost, the Boxer is a thinking dog. He is always thinking of the next thing to do! If he can't reach something on the worktop, then he will work out the best way to get it. Standing on his hind legs is no problem for this athletic breed, so it's better to be safe than sorry and keep the Sunday roast out of reach!

A friend of mine had cooked a joint of beef to make roast beef sandwiches for tea. Before she left for work, she asked her husband to switch off the oven and hang out the washing. When she returned some time later, she looked in the oven for the beef and it had gone. Calling her husband for an explanation, he could give her no answer, except that before he went to hang out the washing, he had left the oven door slightly ajar for the beef to cool while he was in the garden. On his return, he had pushed the door shut. He had not checked that the beef was still there! In fact, it was in their 10-year-old Boxer, who lay curled in his basket, snoring gently, with a satisfied smile on his face!

behaviour to gain your attention.

Of course, where the Boxer is a family member, he will be busy for most of the day, either helping his owner with the gardening or getting into mischief with the children! Boxers need exercise and mental stimulation to stop them from becoming bored.

Never exercise a Boxer just after his dinner. This is because, in common with many deep-chested breeds, he is prone to bloat, a potentially fatal condition, which is often aggravated by drinking copious amounts of water on top of a large meal. For this reason alone, exercise your Boxer before feeding and allow him to cool down before he has his meal. For more information on bloat, see Chapter Eight: Happy and Healthy.

TEMPERAMENT

The Boxer is fearless and self-assured, though he is often distrustful of strangers until he has been properly introduced. He is quick to recognise friend from foe and responds immediately to friendly overtures. Always quick to sound the alarm when visitors arrive, he soon settles once he realises there is no threat to his family. Generally speaking, the Boxer is not a noisy dog, allowing regular callers, like the milkman and the postman, to come and go unheralded, as he knows they pose no threat.

The Boxer is protective of his family, preferring to put himself between the family members and the source of danger than take up an aggressive stance. He is

14

trustworthy and stoical with young children; he is tolerant of their probing fingers, never snapping or growling. When he has had enough and desires some peace and quiet, he will merely get up and remove himself to his bed. This is a highly intelligent breed that is quick to learn, (often things that you might not want him to, like opening doors!). He needs to keep busy, and will be only too happy to join the children in his family in getting up to mischief.

Boxers are not for the faint-hearted, as they are playful and enthusiastic, throwing themselves into family life with great enthusiasm, and remaining like a puppy well into old age.

When new toys are brought into our house, our 14-year-old bitch snatches each one first and charges off down the garden, with the dogs in hot pursuit, only allowing them to play with the toy when she has become bored.

I don't know whether it is a particular Boxer trait, but every Boxer I have ever owned always greets me with a 'present' when I have been away for some time. Usually this takes the form of a shoe or toy; the dog brings the gift to me, wagging not just his tail but the whole of his body, and the more enthusiastically I thank him, the harder he wags his tail! One of my older males is a bit slow in getting up and if a

present is not immediately to hand, he drags both his blanket and basket to me for my approval.

TRAINABILITY
A Boxer is very easy to train, as he is very intelligent and anxious to please. Training can begin as soon as you bring your new puppy home – there is much to learn! A pup learns quickly, but he is easily bored if the exercise is continually repeated. Be patient and keep your training sessions short – about 10-15 minutes – and intersperse lessons with fun and games. Remember to praise lavishly when your dog gets things right and ignore any mistakes.

The Boxer is an intelligent dog, and if his mind is not kept occupied, he will find his own mischief.

Be consistent and do not move on to the next exercise until you are sure that he has grasped the previous one, as this will lead to confusion. All dogs should be taught at least the very basics of obedience, which will make them much better dogs to live with, and could save their lives under extreme circumstances.

Basic commands, such as "Come", "Sit", "Down" and "Stay", should be taught to your dog. It is often a good idea to join a local dog training class where you will get the stimulus of different types of dogs and owners, and it will also help to socialise with different breeds, which is most important, especially in their early months. For more information, see Chapter Six: Training and Socialisation.

AN IDEAL HOME

A Boxer needs lots of space, so a flat or apartment is not ideal. However, if you have plenty of open spaces or parks close by, and you have the time to take your Boxer out for walks, then it can be workable. The ideal environment would be a house with access to a large garden where he can run freely and play with the family members. Living in the country is the perfect location for a Boxer, but they live happily in the town too, so long as exercise is plentiful.

LIVING WITH OTHER ANIMALS

In common with most bull breeds, Boxers are very 'matey' with other dogs, and will accept most other animals if carefully introduced. We are often asked if a puppy will get on with a resident cat or another dog in their new home, and the reply has to be: yes, as long as they are carefully introduced. All that is needed is time and patience.

Cats are usually put out when the new kid on the block arrives,

This is a breed that loves to be part of the family, and is entirely trustworthy with children.

If you are careful with early introductions, a Boxer and a cat will live in harmony.

but a cat will climb up high, keeping out of the puppy's way, and the pup will soon learn to respect this and leave the cat alone. Some of our owners report that their cat and puppy even sleep together and groom each other.

I was once given an adult Persian cat and my seven adult Boxers that all lived in the house were avid cat chasers, not even allowing the neighbour's cats to sit on the garden fence! Great care had to be taken for the first few days, but after a week of standoff, everyone relaxed; the cat was accepted and harmony returned – but they still chased the neighbour's cats!

When my elderly parents lost their 13-year-old Boxer, they felt they couldn't give the time to a baby puppy, so I found them a five-year-old male called Flash Gordon, who certainly lived up to his name! My parents had four

cats and the moment Flash entered the kitchen, mayhem ensued, with chairs and kitchen table, complete with the Sunday dinner, flying across the floor. We skidded across the floor in gravy and Brussel sprouts, up to our necks in spitting, hissing cats! Mum said, "That dog has got to go." He never did, of course, and within a couple of weeks he could be found snoozing on the sofa surrounded by four furry hot-water bottles.

His previous owner had omitted to tell us that Flash Gordon was an avid cat chaser. He had once been out on a walk when a cat shot past him, and as his lady owner clung on to his lead like grim death, he hurtled through a hedge like a thunderbolt, only to find a family enjoying a picnic on the other side. Flash dragged her gleefully through the middle of the gathering, scattering people,

custard tarts and cups of tea in his wake with his red-faced owner, now bedecked with twigs and leaves, apologising profusely. The thrill for Flash was in the chase. Once the cat stood still, so did he – thankfully!

I have a number of friends that keep other breeds of dogs with Boxers, and they all seem to get on well. We had a Lhasa Apso for 13 years, and she ruled the roost here. If the Lhasa was on one of the dog beds and a Boxer wanted to lie down, she only had to give a look, and the Boxer would slink off to find somewhere else to have a snooze. The Lhasa Apso has a big personality in a little dog's body, and the Boxers accepted her authority implicitly.

When I was quite young I had a New Zealand white rabbit that I used to take for a walk on a lead, and my Boxer loved him. Later on, when my children came along, we had a cockatiel that

This is an exuberant breed, and jumping seems to come naturally.

was a great talker. One of our Boxers, called Cher, was fixated by the cockatiel and used to press her muzzle against the cage while the cockatiel squawked loudly in protest and pecked furiously at her nose. Cher never flinched. I really thought that she had designs on a cockatiel dinner, but one day when the cockatiel escaped from his cage she caught him and brought him to me. She gently put him on my lap, completely unscathed, whereupon

he launched a tirade of abuse at her, obviously very angry to have his freedom curtailed!

This all proves that, with careful supervised introductions, Boxers are very tolerant and will accept almost any other pet.

CLOWN DOGS

Boxers are very boisterous dogs, and this love of life does tend to get them unwittingly into trouble. This, coupled with their natural curiosity and the ability to think

for themselves, often leads them into hilarious situations. The look on a Boxer's face when he is admonished for wrongdoing is priceless, causing the owner to dissolve into helpless laughter. One of my earliest memories is dressing our dogs up in shorts, T-shirts and sunglasses, and then rolling around on the floor with laughter. No problem there, a Boxer doesn't mind being laughed at, as long as he is the centre of attention.

There is always great excitement among my Boxers when I am planting out new bedding plants in the spring. They follow me from place to place, pushing their muzzles into the wet, black peat, playing tug-of-war with the plastic rubbish sacks and shredding them to ribbons, then trotting off with the polystyrene trays, taking great delight in dismembering them until the garden looks like a scene from White Christmas. Once finished, when it is time to go inside for a well-earned cup of tea, I have hardly sat down and started dunking my rich tea biscuits when, without fail, in trots one of the Boxers, head held high with obvious pride, dangling a precious bedding plant, complete with roots, dripping dollops of wet black peat all over the carpet, while his whole body wags with delight – "Look, Mum, I've brought you a present!"

HEAD-ON COLLISION

Jumping up comes naturally to a Boxer, probably harking back to his early bull-baiting ancestors who had to leap up and grip the bull by the nose. This natural trait manifests itself when greeting owners, whether they have been gone for several hours or even minutes – and this can often result in a sore nose or chin. It is wise to teach your young puppy to sit while you go down to his level to greet him, otherwise he will meet you on the way up, and the clash of heads can be a tad uncomfortable!

If your Boxer is bored, he will soon find ways to keep himself amused.

Boxer's chins and heads are very hard. I know this to my cost, as one evening I had one of my dogs sitting on my lap (yes, a Boxer makes a great lap dog; if there is not enough lap to go around, a Boxer doesn't mind hanging over the edges), and the whole family was watching TV. I said to my husband, "You know, Dolly is one of the most loving, gentle Boxers we have ever owned." Hardly had the words left my mouth when the doorbell rang. Dolly threw her head back and barked, but in doing so, she hit me in the mouth with her head. I fell on the floor, as the pain was excruciating, while the whole family erupted in hysterical laughter, tears rolling down their faces. Dolly stood over me with a quizzical look on her face. She was unhurt, but I had to go for emergency dental treatment to have my front tooth splinted back into position at 10pm that night.

WAIT AND SEE!

In my early days of owning Boxers, I didn't have a car crate, so I trained the dogs to "Wait" as I opened the tailgate of the car. They would sit patiently until I told them it was OK, and then they would leap out and rush off into the field for their walk. I felt I had got this down to a fine art, so one Sunday afternoon I drove down the lane and parked in the gateway of the field where I normally exercised the dogs. As I got out of the car, I saw a family taking an afternoon stroll up the lane, and being very keen to show off my training skills, I waited until they were quite close, so they would get a good view of just how obedient my dogs were. Big mistake! The Boxers were desperate for their walk, and by hanging around at the back of the car, I had wound them to a frenzy of excitement. Glancing over my shoulder to ensure I had the

With good care and training, the Boxer is an outstanding family companion.

walkers' attention, I slowly lifted the tailgate, saying, "Wait! Wait!" Did they wait? They did not! They hurled themselves at the tailgate with the ferocity of a heat-seeking missile, causing it to spring up and whack me on the forehead, sending me flying backwards where I bashed the back of my head on the road! Quite shaken, I picked myself up, closed the tailgate and before the concerned audience could enquire as to my wellbeing, I tottered unsteadily into the field as if this circus was an everyday occurrence! The dogs were racing around in great delight, already halfway across the field. It was not quite the impression that I had hoped to make!

While on this subject, a good dog crate saves a lot of problems if you are going to be travelling around with your Boxer. It keeps him safe and secure, and also prevents damage to your car. I once went to a dog show with my husband, and, at the time, we had a young puppy and her mother with us. Having found a shady spot to park, we went to watch the judging. Some time later there was a tannoy announcement asking if the owner of a silver Ford Mondeo could please return to their car, as the dogs were causing mayhem. Along with many other ringsiders, I tittered and giggled, as I thought of the poor owners returning to their car. Boxers, eh?

Who'd have them! Then a few minutes later, I remembered that we had changed our car the previous day, and we were the very people that owned a silver Mondeo estate! We hared back to the car to find that the headlining had been ripped down, together with all the electric wires for the tail lights. The dogs came out of the car, wagging their tails enthusiastically and panting furiously, having had a wonderful time! Lesson learnt: we bought a crate for the car to keep the little darlings secure.

MISCHIEF MAKERS

Boxers should never be left for hours on end, because they get bored and get into mischief.

Some friends visited us just before Christmas one year, and because they lived a couple of hours away and had a number of Boxers, they had to plan their visit with military precision. They brought four dogs with them, leaving their old girl snoring gently in the front room and two others in the kitchen with bones to chew to keep them occupied.

On their return, they were mystified to see three smiling faces peering out of their front room window as they pulled on to the drive. With sinking hearts, they walked into a scene of devastation. Where to begin? One Boxer had opened the kitchen door, then they had set to work. They managed to knock down the Christmas tree and open some presents, consuming anything edible and spitting out anything they didn't want. They had destroyed the festive poinsettia, taking it (complete with compost and roots) on to the sofa together with a bag of tangerines, which they chewed and spat out, making a sticky black porridge. They had then taken themselves up to mum and dad's bed for a well-earned rest, leaving sticky black paw prints in their wake. Our friends still laugh about it to this day, imagining the dogs cavorting around in party mood.

Life with a Boxer is full of the unexpected.

OBEDIENT – UP TO A POINT...

Coupled with their immense sense of fun, Boxers can often be frustrating, as even some of the most highly trained obedience dog can have an off day. I have witnessed this first hand when watching an obedience demonstration.

The handler threw the dumbbell and sent his dog off to retrieve and the Boxer dashed out smartly and picked it up, pausing to gaze around the ring. (Anybody who has ever owned a Boxer will recognise that look, which clearly says, "What else can I do?") On hearing his handler calling him, he glanced over as if to say, "OK, I can hear you; just give me a minute."

He then proceeded to toss the dumbbell in the air playfully, before trotting round the ring to say hello to anyone who took his fancy! Having cocked his leg up a nearby fencepost, he returned smartly and presented his dumbbell to his red-faced owner while the ringside erupted in gales of laughter.

Yes, you definitely need a sense of humour to live with a Boxer!

THE FIRST BOXERS

Chapter 2

How far back in time we go to find the origin of the Boxer breed it is difficult to say. Before the birth of Christ there were drawings of hunting dogs that could be early ancestors of the Boxer. These dogs were used to hunt bears, bison, boars and the bull. They were called 'Bullenbeisser', coming from the term 'bull biter', or 'Barenbeisser', meaning 'bear biter'. These were big-hearted dogs with broad muzzles, broadly spaced teeth, and wide jaws that could hang on to the prey as it struggled to near exhaustion, so that the hunter could come in for the kill. Not a pretty sight! The ancient fighting dogs possessed many of the characteristics of the Boxer, having great courage and virility. These were times when breeding was for strength and speed and only the fittest survived. Pictures of Bullenbeisser-type dogs can be seen as far back as the 1600s.

SETTING A TYPE

From the 1600s onwards, the dog became more than just a hunter's assistant; he was also valued as a guard and a companion. Three distinct types resulted:

- The heavy Bullenbeisser, which was the large, English-type predecessor of the Mastiff.
- The large hound, which went on to become the Great Dane.
- The small Bullenbeisser, which was the base from which the Bulldog was developed in England. In Germany, the same

The sport of bull baiting was outlawed in the early 1800s.

Alt's Schecken: A white bitch with brindle patches.

Flocki: The first Boxer to be registered in the German Munich stud book.

Ch. Blanka von Argentor: The result of a repeat mating between Tom the Bulldog, and Alt's Schecken.

type was used to develop a more elegant dog than our short, stocky Bulldog. This animal had long, straight front legs so he had the build to be an escort for carriages, as well as being a good guard dog.

Fortunately, the sport of bull baiting was outlawed in the early 1800s, but before this came into effect a group of dog fanciers decided to develop a new breed based on the Bullenbeisser. This new breed was to be suited to a more sporting life; smaller, quicker animals were needed to fight the bull in a tight spot. Up to 1830, it seems that the Bullenbeisser was fawn or brindle with a black mask,

with no mention of the white markings that were to follow. Around this time, the white English Bulldog was taken into Germany and crossed with the Bullenbeisser with the aim of producing a more elegant dog, with longer legs, to act as an escort to the horse and carriage.

THE FIRST BOXERS

A dog from a local pack, whose name has never been recorded, was crossed with a Bullenbeisser called Flora to produce the first Boxer cross known as Lechner's Boxel. Flora, who was brought to Germany from France by George Alt, a German citizen who lived in Munich, was then mated back to

her son to produce a bitch named Alt's Schecken. This bitch was mated to Tom, an outcross owned by Dr Toenniesson, another local breeder who lived in Munich. Tom was a white English Bulldog, who, it is safe to assume, looked very much like the Bulldogs of the last century. He had straight front legs, a good length of neck and a body without exaggeration. The result of the mating between Tom and Alt's Schecken was Flocki, a dark brindle male with flashy white markings, who was born in Munich on 26 February 1895.

Flocki is written as Number 1 in the German Munich stud book. He gained his place in the stud book after winning the Boxer class

24

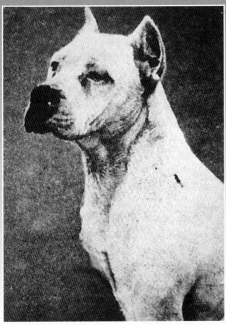

Piccolo von Argentor, sired by Maier's Lord.

Hugo von Pfalzgau: It is thought that many British Boxers are descended from this dog.

put on at a St. Bernard show – he was the first ever Boxer to be shown.

The mating that produced Flocki was repeated, this time to produce Blanka von Argentor. Flora was again mated to Lechner's Boxel and produced Maier's Lord. Maier's Lord went on to sire a white dog called Piccolo von Argenter, and the subsequent mating of Blanka and Piccolo produced Meta von der Passage, who was the real foundation of the breed today. He produced many important Boxers, including Ch. Giggerl and Hugo von Pfalzgau. Giggerl was a dominant brindle and played a large part in reducing the number

of whites in the breed, although obviously we still see this white gene coming through in our litters today. We will see later in this chapter why white dogs were unattractive for certain tasks. Hugo then sired Ch. Kurt von Pfalzgau, who was taken to one of Giggerl's granddaughters to sire Ch. Rolf von Vogelsburg.

This may all seem like a puzzle that you cannot unravel, but what is significant is the amount of inbreeding that went on in the early days to produce the Boxer. However, this was the only way to establish the breed characteristics.

THE FIRST BOXER CLUB
In January 1896 the Munich

Boxer Club was formed, and on 29 March of that year the club held its first show at the home of another enthusiast, Joseph Himmelreich. The judge was Elard Konig, one of three fanciers who promoted the Boxer, along with Friedrich Robert and R. Hopner. Many of the entries were white in colour, some white with patches of brindle and red. Some were black. It was after this show that the members of the club took on the task of producing a Standard for the breed. The first German Breed Standard was adopted on 14 January 1902, following many arguments about what the Boxer should look like. In fact, it resulted in a temporary split in the

Early breed enthusiasts pictured at the first Boxer show in 1896.

club, but members reunited in 1905 to accept what became the Munich Standard.

One of the good things to appear in these early years was the publication of the first stud book in July 1904, along with the first issue of *Boxer Blatter*. This was the first magazine all about our beloved Boxer and it published a lot of early information about the breed.

PIONEERS OF THE BREED

In the early pages of her book, *My Life With Boxers,* Boxer pioneer Friederun Stockmann said she believed that she was destined to spend her life with dogs because she was born in 1891 under Sirius, the Dog Star. At the age of 18, she says, she was led by the Dog Star to Munich where she began her art studies at the Academy in Munich. Unlike her friends who wanted to dance and go to parties, she dreamed of her independence and being able to walk along the lovely avenues of Munich with a good friend – not the two-legged variety, but a four-legged one – a Boxer!

It was in Munich that Friederun met her first Boxer, Pluto. After paying no attention to Philip Stockmann and the other young men at the art night classes she attended, Friederun became interested when Philip told her how his dog had knocked over a lamp as it bounded to meet him. She asked him what type of dog it was, and Philip described the animal as being like a tiger with a big head and a great black muzzle. Friederun realised that this must be a Boxer, and when she met Pluto, she described him as the best-mannered Boxer she had ever seen. However, he did have some unsocial habits in that he was a notorious fighter.

Pluto awakened a thirst for knowledge in Friederun, and after doing some research, she approached Herr Albert Schmoeger (a breeder) to ask if Pluto could be registered and used for breeding. She was delighted to get a positive response. Herr Schmoeger found a six-month-old female for her, called Laska, but on seeing how well she developed, Herr Schmoeger thought she deserved better than Pluto, who Friederun now recognised as a poor specimen.

Friederun returned from college, worrying about her parents' reaction to the dogs, as they were still unaware that they had been helping her to finance the dogs while paying her college fees! She need not have worried, as they fell in love with the two Boxers. Neither of these dogs contributed much to the breed, as Pluto died without ever having been used at stud, and Laska did not produce any quality puppies.

DEVELOPING THE BREED

Friederun and Philip Stockmann married in 1911, and they are renowned throughout the Boxer fraternity as the real groundbreakers for the breed. Philip was always a little unhappy about the name 'Boxer', which he felt was decidedly English, but to have called our breed 'Kampfer', which was the German translation, would have been a tongue-twister for most of us!

Writing in his book, *Derr Boxer,* Philip Stockmann said that: "The English as born breeding geniuses conceived the over typical and grotesque and so produced the present-day Bulldog. The practical Germans, however, did not wish to sacrifice the value of bull-biters to a monstrous external appearance."

After their marriage, the Stockmanns were attending the Munich Show where they heard that Ch. Rolf von Vogelsburg was for sale. He was expensive, but he had been doing well. So, with money they had saved for a house, they bought this handsome dog that would become the foundation of their famous von Dom kennel. The origin of this famous kennel name was thought to be Vom Dom, meaning 'of the cathedral', as Pluto was known to be a brute who would pick fights with other dogs outside the local cathedral.

THE WAR YEARS

There was a growing interest in breeding Boxers, but activities were severely curtailed during the First World War.

Philip Stockmann was called up in 1914, leaving his wife with the words, "I know you will manage." He took 10 of their Boxers with him, and went into the Home Guard to organise the military deployment of these dogs. Many of his friends from the Munich Boxer Club were also called to serve, and in total about 60 dogs were given to the army.

Soon they were at the front line. A number of Boxers were trained to find wounded soldiers. The Boxers would tear off the soldiers' identity tags and take them to the medics, and then lead the medics back to the wounded soldiers.

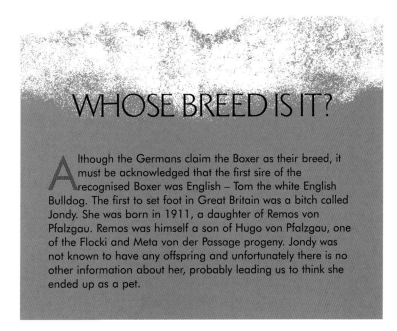

WHOSE BREED IS IT?

Although the Germans claim the Boxer as their breed, it must be acknowledged that the first sire of the recognised Boxer was English – Tom the white English Bulldog. The first to set foot in Great Britain was a bitch called Jondy. She was born in 1911, a daughter of Remos von Pfalzgau. Remos was himself a son of Hugo von Pfalzgau, one of the Flocki and Meta von der Passage progeny. Jondy was not known to have any offspring and unfortunately there is no other information about her, probably leading us to think she ended up as a pet.

One outstanding bitch doing this work was Matthias vom Western, who belonged to Philip Stockmann. She was awarded the Iron Cross, Germany's highest honour, for saving so many lives in this way. It is not clear whether Philip was handling her, or whether she was in the care of another soldier, but she certainly demonstrated tremendous bravery and dedication in very frightening circumstances.

As a result of the success of the Boxer programme, many other breeds were taken on to help the war effort.

THE BLACK BOXER

There were very few Boxer shows between 1914 and 1918, so while Philip was away at war, Friederun concentrated on developing the von Dom line.

She was interested in trying to breed black Boxers, and knew that Edmund Halter, a breeder from Allgaeu, had previously mated a black bitch to Rolf von Vogelsberg. The result had been a beautiful litter of black Boxers, which Friederun was delighted to see. Flock von der Adeleck was the pick of the litter and did well for Herr Halter in the show ring.

Herr Halter wrote to Friederun advising her that he intended to show Flock at a Boxer show at the Nymphenberg Castle in Munich, and asked if she would consider mating Flock to her top-class Rassel vom Dom, who was in season at that time. Friederun agreed to take Flock to the show for him; she groomed him to perfection but was still concerned as to how he looked. She felt the colour on his quarters was not as

Friederun Stockmann pictured with her Boxers in 1914. Ch. Rolf von Vogelsberg is on the extreme right.

deep and decided to improve it with a tin of shoe polish! She started to brush him with the cream polish as a bit of joke, but was so impressed with the effect that she continued until he was gleaming. His owner could not believe the improved appearance, and wished that his wife were able to achieve so much.

Unfortunately, Friederun had worn a beautiful dress of cream Russian silk. She felt the dress would be a stark contrast to the dog – and she was not disappointed. As she walked him to his owner, who would, of course, show the dog, he was close by her all the way. Unfortunately, Herr Halter was forced to point out that Friederun's dress was all black on the left side. Her sins were uncovered! She handed the dog over to his owner and borrowed Herr Halter's coat to cover the marks. She felt guilty and never did anything like that again.

The mating of Flock to Rassel vom Dom took place and Friederun dreamed of three puppies: a brindle, a black male with white markings, and an all-black bitch. Rassel gave birth on her sixty-third day to exactly what Friederun had been praying for – and she felt this was an omen that she was meant to breed black Boxers. Unfortunately, time proved otherwise. In the autumn of 1918, just after the war ended, Munich began to prepare for a new show. Friederun entered her beautiful black Boxers, Ulla and Utter, wanting to show how magnificent these black creatures were.

The only competition Friederun had to fear was from the fawn males. She also entered Rolf, who had just returned from his war service, in the open class for brindles. Utter was also entered in this class, and, as it turned out, Rolf and Utter were the only two entries. Friederun knew that if she didn't show

Rolf, there was a chance for Utter to win the Championship – which would be a first. She was confident that Utter had the quality needed to win, but there are no certainties in showing.

First in the ring was a group of poor-quality fawns. When the time came for the brindles, Friederun entered the ring with Utter; she felt a tension in the atmosphere, which was anything but pleasant. It was only after the event that she found out that the judge had accepted the appointment providing that no first places were awarded to black Boxers. Utter was a strong black dog, with white markings and a white neckband. He showed his socks off, but the breeders in Munich kept silent as they watched to see what would happen. The judge commented that he liked Utter, but his colour was unacceptable. To win first prize he would have to be totally black. This came as a complete shock to Friederun, as the Breed Standard contained no colour definition.

She then brought Rolf into the ring and he was awarded first prize, and his fifth Championship title. The judge marked him as "First Class" and wrote only four words in his critique: "Still the beautiful Rolf." To make his point even more firmly, the judge withdrew the second prize and gave Utter third place. In his critique he wrote, "For the lovers of the black colour, a very nice dog, but he will never have success at a show." Friederun felt that she had been reprimanded; she thought that the judging was unfair and unsporting.

Rassel got her Championship title that day, but this did not ease the disappointment for Friederun. She knew that this would probably mean the end of the strain of black Boxers, and this saddened her. She knew that she could have persevered, but decided that the battle for the black Boxer was not for her.

BETWEEN THE WARS

The great Rolf returned from his war efforts to win another Championship before his death in 1920 at the age of 12 years, but by this time his great-great-great-grandson, Sigurd von Dom was the top stud dog. Sigurd passed on his wonderful qualities consistently to his progeny and it was the right decision to allow him to go to the USA, where he became International Champion Sigurd Von Dom of Barmere.

Back in Germany in 1934, the result of a double-grandfather mating at the von Dom kennels produced Ch. Lustig von Dom, who was also to be a great force in American Boxers.

THE STOCKMANN LEGACY

Philip Stockmann died in a concentration camp hospital in 1945, leaving his wife to keep the von Dom name going, but at the end of the Second World War she had only one remaining granddaughter left to continue the line. However, most of today's

Friederun Stockmann judging Ch. Bang away of Sirrah Crest as a puppy. The Stockmanns devoted their lives to the Boxer breed.

Boxers can be traced back to von Dom.

Friederun Stockmann's book, *My Life with Boxers*, is a remarkable record, and is well worth reading. Perhaps most apt of all is this description: "The Boxer, however, is a gentleman amongst dogs with short coats. He not only wants the best food, he wants to be handled in a civilized manner too. He can easily be upset by his master and this is called being leader-sensitive. He cannot stand a hard hand or injustice. It is true that he is pig-headed and every one has a personality of its own. His real job is to be a house and family dog and to be a friend to the children."

What a wonderful summary of our breed, and one that still holds true today.

AMERICA'S BIG FOUR

Ch. Rolf von Vogelsburg's son, Dampf von Dom, was the first Boxer to be exported to the USA, where he became the first American Champion in 1915. However, the success of the Boxer in the USA can be attributed to four highly influential imports from Germany who producing many Champions between them.

INT. CH. SIGURD VON DOM

One of Rolf's descendants, born in 1925, was Ivein von Dom who, although never a Champion himself, went on to sire the famous Sigurd von Dom. Sigurd remained in Germany for five years and became as renowned a sire and show dog as the great Rolf von Vogelsberg. He was then sold to America to become a part of the Barmere kennels in Van Nuys, California. J.P. Wagner, who was the owner of the Mazelaine kennels and one of the top American breeders, believed that Sigurd had more influence than any other dog for the development of a balance of power and elegance.

CH. LUSTIG VON DOM

Sigurd's grandson, Ch. Lustig von Dom, was also sold to America, and became Ch. Lustig von Dom of Tulgey Woods. This was after achieving the Czechoslovakian Sieger in 1935, Fachschaftssieger (club Champion dog, winner of First Open with rating of Excellent under three different judges),

THE BIG FOUR

Int. Ch. Sigurd von Dom.

Int. Ch. Utz von Dom of Mazelaine.

Int. Ch.Lustig von Dom of Tulgey Wood.

Int. Ch. Dorian von Marienhof of Mazelaine.

German Reichssieger (winner of the annual speciality Championship show, thereby becoming dog Champion of the year) and Weltseiger (World Champion). On arrival in America, he became a Champion within a week and, as in Germany, he was never beaten in his breed. He was shown 20 times, 20 Best of Breed, 12 groups and twice Best in Show all breeds. Lustig was mated to 168 bitches and sired 41 Champions in his lifetime, but also there are a number of German title winners that have never been numbered. He died at the age of 11 in 1945 having left a remarkable legacy on the Boxer breed in Germany, the USA and in Britain.

FIRST BRITISH-BRED LITTER

The first litter born in Great Britain was on 7 February 1930 to a bitch, Cilly von Rothenberg, who was imported in whelp by Patience Rogers. The litter had three surviving dog puppies. The puppies were registered as: Riverhill Rackateer, who was kept by Miss Rogers; the second puppy was registered by Mrs Wills and Captain Cleland as Beginner at Willstud. The third puppy was not registered until 1936, just in time to compete and win at Crufts; he was owned by Gore Graham, and called Willi v. Brandenberg.

DORIAN VON MARIENHOF OF MAZELAINE
The third influential import was Dorian von Marienhof of Mazelaine, another grandson of Sigurd. Dorian was bred by Frau Tehekla Schneider in the East German region of Germany, and sold as a puppy to a butcher. He became a sensation in his day, and when he won the International Seiger title in 1936, he was spotted by Mazie Wagner of the Mazelaine prefix. She begged to buy the dog but was refused. She sent a telegram to the butcher, offering 4,000 dollars, and this time her bid was successful. In 1936 when Dorian was imported to the USA, he went straight to the top and won the Working Dog Group at Westminster Kennel Club Show in 1937.

CH. UTZ VON DOM
The quartet of influential imports was completed when Ch. Utz von Dom, Lustig's brother, arrived in the USA. He was imported by the Wagners in 1939 and was a great show dog and sire. He followed Dorian to become the second Boxer to win the group at Westminster. But his greatest claim to fame was through his son, Ch. Warlord of Mazelaine. Born in October 1942, this fawn dog won the Working Group three years running at the Westminster Show (1945-1947), going on to win Best in Show at Westminster in 1947, which was a first for Boxers.

FIRST BRITISH BOXERS
Before the First World War few people in Britain were interested in the Boxer breed. In 1933 Mrs Cecil Sprigge brought a red dog from Paris, sired by Armin von der Haake. He was registered as Fritz of Leith Hill. In 1934 she brought in a young Dutch brindle bitch, Kralingen's Liesel, who was sired by Ch. Armin Edelblut. Mrs Sprigge, who was responsible for persuading Charlie Cruft to schedule Boxer classes at Crufts in 1936, also imported from Germany Gretl von der Boxerstadt, who was in whelp to Hansl von Biderstein, a descendant of Causer von Deutenkofen. Gretl produced the first British-bred Champion, Ch. Horsa of Leith Hill. He became a Champion in 1936, winning Challenge Certificates at Blackpool, Richmond and Kensington, and Best of Breed at Crufts in 1937, 1938 and 1939.

Ch. Horsa of Leith Hill: The first British Boxer Champion.

Kaspar of Fieldburcote: This Boxer served in the British army in the Second World War.

Unfortunately, the effects of the Second World War prevented him from having a major impact on the breed.

Allon Dawson was also an influential member of the Boxer fraternity, importing a bitch who was in whelp to Lustig von Dom. This produced two Challenge Certificate winners for the Stainburndorf kennels. He also owned the Lustig son, Zuntfig von Dom, bringing that line of breeding to the UK. Unfortunately, due to the war, Zuntfig was shipped off to the USA, strengthening the breed there and leaving the UK behind.

INFLUENTIAL BLOODLINES

In 1938 Elizabeth Somerfield (Panfield) saw a well-constructed bitch with a wonderful temperament and good colour, Gretl von der Boxerstadt. She liked her so much that in 1939 she bought one of Gretl's daughters, sired by Fritz of Leith Hill. The bitch, called Annaliese, was the first of the Panfield Boxers. As the country was going to war, dogs were in plentiful supply, prices were low and in May 1940 Elizabeth Somerfield and Mary Davis bought Gretl von der Boxerstadt for £5 in partnership. They decided to mate her and happened to meet a Boxer owner while they were travelling in Hampshire. His dog was a grandson of the wonderful Sigurd, Ajax von Muhlenburg.

The litter that Gretl and Ajax produced consisted of a red dog and two red bitches. The bitch became Panfield Astra, and she was to be the foundation bitch of the Gremlin kennels after being bought by Marion Fairbrother.

Astra was mated to Zulu, the Zunftig son, and Panfield Flak was the result. Flak went off to Germany where he was bought by an American officer and was then taken back to the USA. Flak was the sire of Ch. Panfield Tango, who was the leading British Boxer during 1949 and 1950, but was subsequently exported to Australia. Unfortunately, on his arrival there, Tango fell into the ship's hold and broke his hind legs. Mrs Gerardy, his owner, insisted a vet try to save him and delicate surgery was done on his legs, which were pinned and plastered. Tango had a chair on wheels and he could propel himself along on this contraption – what a sight to behold! He made a good recovery and went on to sire several Champions. Tango's dam was one of the foundation bitches in the Panfield kennel from 1947.

Gremlin Gunner was another in the litter from Gretl and Ajax; he went on to win two Challenge Certificates after the war. The third pup in the litter was Mutineer of Maspound. He sired a Champion, Ch. Monarchist of Maspound. M Guthrie was the owner of Monarchist and Mutineer. In 1946 when J.P. Wagner came over from the USA to judge and award the first Challenge Certificates after the war, Monarchist won his first CC and Best of Breed. Wagner was reported to say that his greatest disappointment was in the bulkiness of the UK dogs, with wide fronts, heavy shoulders and quite light hindquarters. The Americans had been lucky with the 'Big Four' and Wagner felt that in the UK we had lost sight of the fact that this was a working breed that should be able to jump high fences and run at great speed for long distances. British breeders took this on board and with the use of imports went on to develop a more typical Boxer.

Two Champions from the early 1950s: Ch. Toplocks Welladay of Sheafdon (left) and her son Ch. Sheafdon Spellmaker sired by the American inport Mazelaine's Texas Ranger.

POST-WAR BOXERS

After the Second World War, the arrival of Alma von der Frankenwarte, daughter of the wonderful Lustig von Dom, was to have an impact on the British Boxer. Alma had previously been mated four times without success. She was owned by Elizabeth Somerfield, Mary Davis and Marion Fairbrother, and after being mated to Monkswood Christian of Ramblings, who was a son of Gretl by Fritz of Leith Hill, she produced Britain's first Boxer bitch Champion. Ch. Panfield Serenade gained her title in 1947, and was bred and owned by Elizabeth Somerfield.

Some said Serenade needed more 'stop', but with her overall quality this did not prevent her from winning five Challenge Certificates. She was mated to her half-brother, Panfield Tango, and produced two Champions: Panfield Ringleader and Panfield Rhythm, who won a total of 17 Challenge Certificates between them! Ringleader was a great sire in Britain, siring seven Champions, six others won Challenge Certificates, giving a grand total of 40 Challenge Certificates from his offspring. He also had eight grandchildren who became Champions.

SIGNIFICANT IMPORTS

Some of those who brought influence to the British Boxer in the 1950s were Dutch Ch. Holger von Germania, who sired four Champions, and Dutch Ch. Favourite vom Haus Germania. The famous Wardrobes kennels were heavily influenced by the Dutch breeding of Ch. Winkinglight Justice and Viking. Marion Fairbrother and Martin Summers (Summerdale) brought in Ch. Rainey Lane Sirrocco from the USA in 1958, and he sired 13 Champions. Joan McClaren's Braxburn kennel was

Ch. Seefeld Picasso: Winner of 24 Challenge Certificates and a highly influential sire.

Southern Counties Show 1960: The bitch CC winner (left) is Ch. Wardrobes Silhouette of Arnogor, handled by Connie Wiley. The dog CC winner is Ch. Felcign Hot Cargo handled by Felicia Price. The judge is Jean Haggie (Sheafdon).

also founded on Winkinglight stock.

Ivor and Marion Ward-Davis imported Kreyons Back in Town of Winuwuk back in the 1970s, followed by Winuwuk Milray's Red Baron of Valvay – both dogs brought success to their kennel, and are behind many of the UK pedigrees today.

Pat Heath (Seefeld), through a combination of Winkinglight and Dutch imports, bred Ch. Seefeld Holbein who in the 1960s was the only Show Champion who was also qualified for working trials. He was to be the sire of the famous Ch. Seefeld Picasso, who went on to sire 18 UK Champions and 58 Champions worldwide. The long list of Seefeld Champions over the decades speaks for itself, and reflects the use of American bloodlines.

Some of the dominant sires in the 1980s were Ch. Tyegarth Famous Grouse, Ch. Gremlin Summer Storm and Ch. Starmark Sweet Talkin Guy.

THE CURRENT SCENE

Coming up to date in the UK Boxer world, there are many successful kennels – Faerdorn, Manic, Maranseen, Marbelton, Mindenwood, Newlaithe, Norwatch-Sunhawk, Seacrest, Skelder, Sulez, Walkon, and Winuwuk, to name just a few.

The breeder and owner of the breed record holder, Sue Drinkwater, is a fellow committee member of the British Boxer Club. Sulez Black Magic is the most beautiful bitch you could ever wish for. She currently has 54 Challenge Certificates, 33 Best of Breeds, and 28 Reserve Challenge Certificates. At the age of six, she has just taken time out to produce her first litter – hopefully some very promising progeny for the future!

BOXER REGISTRATIONS

It is interesting to see the growth of Boxer registrations with the Kennel Club and how rapidly the breed grew in popularity. With 399 Boxers registered in 1945, the numbers jumped to 1,412 in 1947, 3,647 in 1950, and 6,054 by 1954. In 2006 the number of Boxers registered with the Kennel Club was 9,006. This was a fall over the previous two years of 9,566 in 2005, and 9,869 in 2004. However, the Boxer has remained solidly at number 9 in the list of the top 20 most popular breeds in the UK and sits at number 6 in the US list.

It will be interesting to see whether the breed registrations fall away with the British ban on tail docking, as many breeders are stating they will not breed Boxers if they cannot dock the tails. Those who are committed to the Boxer will, I am sure, continue with this wonderful breed!

The Boxer has achieved great success in the show ring and is also a favourite among pet owners.

Breed recordholder Ch. Sulez Black Magic pictured with her owner/breeder Sue Drinkwater.

Ch. Walkon Made 'n' Issue: A fine representative from the Walkon kennel.

A BOXER FOR YOUR LIFESTYLE

Chapter 3

The decision to add a canine member to your family is one of the most important you will make, and therefore has to be given a lot of thought. The Kennel Club in the UK tries to help people by holding Discover Dogs at Crufts in March and also in London in November each year. This gives those considering a dog the opportunity to look at a wonderful selection of pedigree dogs found in the UK, and the chance to talk to owners about the pros and cons of each breed.

Those who visit the Boxer stand always have smiles on their faces, as the Boxer is renowned for being the canine clown. Boisterous and full of fun, the Boxer never seems to grow up and will want to play well into his old age. Do not be fooled by that small bundle of energy you see as a puppy – that cute little thing will grow into a powerful dog that needs careful training and handling. Yes, a Boxer will make a great family pet and he will be a faithful companion, but he will also demand a lot of attention and a great deal of exercise.

MAKING THE COMMITMENT

Before making the commitment to purchase a Boxer, you must give full consideration to the change this will make to your lifestyle for the next 10 to 12 years, and be absolutely sure you are happy to cope with these changes.

HOW WILL A BOXER FIT INTO YOUR DAILY ROUTINE?

A Boxer is a dog who needs company, and he will not cope with being left on his own for long periods of time. This may be a problem if you work full-time, unless you have a willing relative or neighbour who would be happy to come to your home and take the dog for walks or supervise while he plays in the garden several times during the day. There may be a local dog-walking service that can provide someone who will come to your home and take the dog for a walk. What you cannot expect to do is to go off to work all day, leaving your Boxer pup unattended.

The Boxer is an energetic breed who needs and loves exercise in equal measure. If a Boxer is left unattended in the home for long periods of time, he will be bored and potentially destructive. House training will be almost impossible if the puppy does not have the opportunity to go outside regularly to relieve himself. You will find most respectable breeders will be reluctant to sell a puppy if you work full-time and the dog will be alone all day.

When you take on a Boxer, you are responsible for his needs for the duration of his life.

DO YOU HAVE TIME FOR A BOXER?

Right from the time you first go to see a litter of puppies, you will quickly appreciate that the Boxer is very time-consuming. I sit for hours, watching a new litter of puppies and mum caring for them. You need to be prepared to sacrifice other things to make time for your new member of the family. A new puppy will need feeding four times a day and will need regular exercise.

I remember being told that a Boxer needs seven miles of walking a day to keep in shape, but this was a slight exaggeration, thank goodness! A good walk at least two or three times a day should suffice, as long as the dog also has the opportunity to play freely in your garden. Free-running exercise is a delight to a Boxer, particularly if he can chase a ball or a Frisbee.

THE POWER TO DESTROY

Take care to ensure that you buy toys that are not easily destroyed, and never leave a Boxer unattended with a toy unless you are sure that there are no small parts that he can swallow. Raggies or solid rubber toys are the best option. Boxers can destroy supposedly indestructible toys easily, in a very short space of time.

Hide chews may also be recommended, but these are an absolute no-no to a Boxer! He will keep on gnawing until the chew becomes soft and pliable, and then swallow the lot. The result can often be a trip to the vet for surgery. Give him a nice knucklebone and he will chew for hours, although if it is a really greasy one, it may make his bowel movements loose for a few days!

CAN YOU MAKE YOUR HOME BOXER-PROOF?

You will need to prepare your home before bringing a new puppy, or even an older Boxer, home. No more leaving newspapers and remote controls on the floor, as your pup will assume they are for him to chew. If you have stairs in the home, then investing in a child safety gate is a good idea. Allowing a Boxer puppy to climb stairs may look cute as he struggles up and down, but it is not good for his construction. A puppy's bones are still soft and many a good show prospect has had his front ruined by being allowed to climb stairs.

Your dog should have his own place to sleep in a separate room to the family, such as the kitchen area, in a crate or a rubber dog bed. A nice wicker basket looks great, but will not survive a Boxer's teeth for very long. Make sure your dog is not left within easy reach of woodwork that can be chewed – this is where the crate comes in really useful!

You may have decided to build outside kennelling for your dog. If this is the case, then ensure it is fully enclosed and escape-proof. The Boxer is not as dumb as people may think, and I have

Holidays will be even more fun if you can take your Boxer with you – but if this is not possible, you will need to make suitable arrangements.

known many dogs who are expert escapologists and think nothing of clearing a five-foot fence!

You will also need to ensure that the kennel and run has a concrete base so that Boxer cannot dig his way out. Fit padlocks on external gates and pen doors to be sure the dog cannot escape and to prevent theft.

WHAT HAPPENS WHEN YOU GO ON HOLIDAY?

If you own a dog, it is not so easy to go on holiday. You cannot just go off for a weekend with friends, or even stay out overnight after a party. Make enquiries about local boarding kennels to help with this. Find out what facilities are available, how dogs are fed and exercised,

CRATE NEWS

Boxers make wonderful pets, but they will become destructive if they are bored. My first Boxer was left unattended and free to roam the lounge and kitchen area; I came home to find a houseplant trashed and the soil well trodden into the carpet. I very quickly purchased my first dog crate! You may be concerned at reading this, but the Boxer appreciates that when he is put in the crate, it is a place to be quiet and relax. The crate becomes his shelter, and if children are becoming too demanding, a Boxer will take himself off into the crate to escape any teasing.

There is nothing unkind about putting a Boxer in the right-sized crate for moderate periods of time. He may cry at first, but he will soon get used to the routine as long as the period in the crate is not too long. This can help with house training too, as a dog will rarely foul his own bed. You should also consider having an appropriate car crate for travelling, as this will keep your dog safe and the crate will protect him from injury.

what vaccinations are required, and you will also want to know what it will cost.

Listen to recommendations from friends, but go and see a boarding establishment for yourself so that you are happy with the surroundings your pet will be in while you are away from him. Most kennels insist on seeing vaccination cards and many ask for kennel cough vaccination. Boxers do not like having this vaccine, which is puffed up the nose, but it prevents the most serious form of kennel cough, which is known as bordetella. The symptoms of this condition are very distressing and to be avoided at all costs.

Another solution may be a pet sitter, who will come into your home and care for the dog while also looking after your home. Or you may prefer to find someone who takes the dog into their own home.

In all cases, you must be sure that you can trust the person with your dog, and be confident that the dog will be happy with them.

WHAT DO YOU WANT FROM YOUR BOXER?

Now that you are aware of the impact on your lifestyle, you need to know what you want from your Boxer – a pet, a show dog, a working dog, a male or a female?

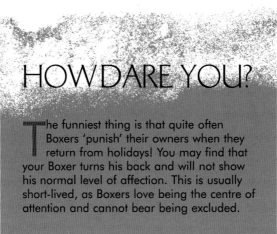

HOW DARE YOU?

The funniest thing is that quite often Boxers 'punish' their owners when they return from holidays! You may find that your Boxer turns his back and will not show his normal level of affection. This is usually short-lived, as Boxers love being the centre of attention and cannot bear being excluded.

SHOW BOXERS

My first experience of having a Boxer was when a puppy was given to my husband for his birthday when we got married. We collected the puppy, and we were told that he was good enough to show. I said I didn't believe in all of that nonsense, but the seed was sown in my subconscious. We went to a village fete when the puppy was six months old and entered him into a companion dog show just for fun. When he won 'Most Handsome Dog', I was hooked and decided that I would learn more about showing.

Now, 18 years later, I have five adult Boxers – four bitches, and one dog – all related! I only breed when I want a new puppy to show, which is about every two years. I have made a huge circle of friends in the show world, but it is an expensive hobby that involves a lot of travelling up and down the country. The highlight

for me was winning a first at Crufts in 2003!

To show dogs, you need to be fairly robust and take the bad luck with the good. Many hours have to be spent training the dog and a lot goes into training the owner – that means you! It is essential to enrol in a good ringcraft class where you will learn how to show. Show entries and travelling can be expensive and you need to be sure that you can afford this investment before venturing into showing. You will find, however, that you will be given lots of help and advice by those who are involved and you will always have someone to talk to.

WORKING BOXERS

Boxers are not thought of as natural obedience or agility dogs, but those who do this with their animals will tell you how wonderful it can be. You need patience and you will need to attend the necessary training for both obedience and agility. But Boxers love the challenge, and will give their heart and soul to do well for their handlers.

The British Boxer Club runs two Open shows and one Championship show each year, as well as a Working Day for Boxers in September. This covers Boxer racing (they love that!), agility, obedience, and an all-breeds companion dog show to raise

The agile Boxer loves taking part in sport and games, and white Boxers, who are excluded from the show ring, often compete with distinction.

money for charitable causes.

White Boxers are regular competitors at these events and it is wonderful to see them working so well. White Boxers cannot be shown because their colouring does not conform to the Breed Standard, but they can compete in obedience and agility competitions and, of course, they make excellent pets.

DOG OR BITCH?

The decision about whether to have a dog or a bitch quite often comes down to personal preference, but there can also be physical reasons for choosing one or the other. Boxers are strong animals and the male will be more so. A Boxer who is out of control on a lead is not a pretty sight, and you should ensure

your puppy is trained to walk to heel from a very early stage. If you have a bitch, then you will have her seasons to cope with. Not only can this be unpleasant, coping with stains on your floors so that you are constantly following her cloth in hand, but the bitch becomes attractive to males of all breeds! This makes walking the bitch difficult.

The male (left) is larger and more powerful than the female.

However, if you are considering a puppy for the show ring, then I would suggest a bitch would be best. If she is a pretty bitch but does not quite make the standard to do well, you can breed from her, using a good stud dog, and hopefully produce something better to show. If you have a dog puppy that doesn't make the grade, then you are stuck with no way to progress your line.

FINDING A PUPPY

Now that you are sure about what you want from your Boxer, the search for your new puppy begins – but where do you start? Finding a reputable breeder is the best option, where you should have the opportunity to see the litter and the mother. You may also be able to see the sire, as some kennels use their own males at stud to maintain a particular line, but this is not always the case. Breeders often want to use the stud dog that has been doing well in the show ring, particularly if they know that he is producing good stock and they are hoping to breed a good show puppy.

When a breeder has a litter, the prime purpose is not to have puppies to sell, but to rear a puppy for the show ring. This is likely to mean that the sire and dam are of excellent quality stock and should produce nice puppies. The breeder will probably only want to keep one or two from the litter, and this leaves the remaining puppies for sale to good homes.

You may want a bitch to breed from, but if you do not intend to breed from her, then you would be well advised to let her have at least one or two seasons naturally, and then consider having her spayed. The down side can be that she may be more prone to putting on weight and you will have to monitor her diet after spaying. Your vet will explain what is involved in spaying and the cost, which is not routinely covered under pet insurance. Boxer bitches do not necessarily have a season every six months, but can go anything from six months up to a year between seasons.

You may decide you want a bitch, as you think she will be more loving and biddable. This is not necessarily the case; the male Boxer can be just as loving.

MAKING CONTACT

Details of reputable breeders can be found by contacting breed club secretaries, who will often know where there are puppies in the area and can give basic advice on buying a puppy. The details of the secretary in your area can be obtained from the Kennel Club. The Kennel Club in the UK and the American Kennel Club in the USA can also provide details of breeders who have registered a litter for sale on their puppy register, but this is no guarantee of quality and you must be careful to vet any breeder fully by asking the right questions.

Be wary of anyone offering to bring the puppy to you, rather than allowing you to see his home. This can mean that the seller is a puppy farmer who breeds litters purely for profit without caring for the welfare of breeding stock or the puppies produced. In all cases, it is important to see the environment in which the puppies have been raised.

Visiting local dog shows and talking to breeders is another way of getting to know more about this breed. Boxer owners are always keen to talk about their breed!

KENNEL-REARED PUPPIES

I have heard it said that you should never consider a kennel-reared puppy, but I have to disagree with this suggestion. Before starting to breed, I had three puppies that came from reputable breeders who housed their show dogs in kennels, and the puppies were born in a whelping pen at the side of the kennels. These puppies were, in fact, better cared for than some I have seen reared in a home environment. More important is the way the litter has been reared and the care and attention given to the puppies, rather than the location of the whelping box. A reputable breeder will have invested a lot of time and care into the health of the mother and the rearing of the litter, regardless of whether they are in kennels or indoors.

If a breeder has taken time to socialise the litter, there is no need to discount puppies reared in a kennel environment.

It is important to see the mother with her puppies so you get some idea of the temperament they are likely to inherit.

thinning of the coat after whelping, so do not be distressed if mum shows patches of hair loss, as this is usually a sign that she has given everything she can to her pups. She will normally stay with the pups until they have been weaned, but will be taken away from them at around five or six weeks, so that they learn to fend for themselves. We usually still put mum back with her pups at night until six or seven weeks of age. By the time they go off to their new home at eight weeks, they are content without her there.

CHOOSING A PUPPY

You will want to know how many puppies are in the litter, what sex they are and whether any puppies have already been booked. With Boxers there is also the consideration of colour – red or brindle. Most Boxers will have a white chest and they may have white facial markings – or occasionally there will be puppies that are all white.

Be aware that a Boxer that is completely white may sometimes have problems such as deafness. (Deafness can also occur in coloured puppies, although it is much less likely.) Ask if this has been checked out and if the puppy is old enough; ask if you can see for yourself that the puppy reacts to sound. This will not be possible until about six weeks of age when the pups are running around. You should ask if the puppy can be separated from his littermates and taken into another room to see if he

VIEWING A LITTER

Once you have details of the litters available to you, make appointments to see several litters. Boxers are so adorable that it is hard to resist the first puppies you see, and you will probably want to take them all home. Take care, however, to ask the owner lots of questions.

The first thing you will want to know is if both parents have been heart tested and that they are graded a 0 or a 1. This will not guarantee that your puppy will be free of aortic stenosis (heart

murmurs), but will give a better chance that he will be clear. Boxers are not routinely tested for hip dysplasia, but some breeders do so and this is further useful information. If it is possible to see both parents, so much the better, but you will at least wish to see the mother. Ask if other relatives of the bitch are available to see. Viewing a family line of healthy Boxers will give you more confidence in the breeder.

THE MOTHER

Most nursing dams will have

reacts to a sudden noise. There is also the option of having a Baer test as this is the only sure way of knowing if the puppy is deaf. Deafness itself may not prevent you from wanting a particular puppy, but it needs extra-special care in teaching the dog obedience through handsignals rather than sounds. This is time-consuming, but very rewarding if you can do it.

White Boxers are adorable, but you do have the additional task of keeping their faces clean under the eyes. All dogs secrete a fluid that can stain, but it is particularly evident in white Boxers. Wiping daily with an appropriate cleaner can prevent bad staining, however.

THE COST

An important point for many owners is how much a Boxer puppy will cost – and this is a minefield. In 2007, the average price for a puppy in the UK was around £650, but there will be some who sell them cheaper and some who charge anything up to £1,500 for a puppy, particularly a red one. White puppies are usually cheaper at around £300.

No one knows what the effect of the tail docking ban will be. Boxers with tails have not been popular while there was a choice, so prices could drop initially and breeders may find it difficult to sell their puppies with tails. However, if some breeders move away from the breed and numbers of litters drop, then the price may go up again. Pricing is often based on demand.

THE GRILLING

Your top priority should not be price, but to find a reputable breeder who cares deeply for the breed and rears each litter with the utmost care and attention. Do not be surprised when you find yourself on the receiving end of a lot of questions, as any decent breeder will want to know all about you and your family. A breeder will ask about your home, the security of your garden, and whether you have time to look after and exercise a Boxer.

The breeder will also ask if the puppy is to be brought up with children. Boxers are wonderful with children, but no animal should be left unattended with youngsters. A child can tug a dog in a sensitive place – and any dog will react. This does not mean a Boxer is dangerous, merely that he does not like to be hurt any more than we do. Children need to be trained to respect the dog, and to allow him to have his space and his quiet time. They should also be shown how to help with the dog's care, so that they value the relationship they have with their pet.

Raising a family and a Boxer together is a great combination. Many a child has been saved by an alert Boxer who has raised the alarm in time for the parent to prevent an accident. Children of show families like to get involved in junior handling and this can be a very rewarding hobby for a child.

If you are tempted by a white puppy, make sure his hearing has been checked out.

How do you choose which is the right puppy for you?

The breeder will help you to assess whether a puppy has show potential.

ASSESSING PUPPIES

Now you are off to see your first litter – what should you be looking for? Depending on the age of the puppies, you will see different things. The best time to see a litter is once they are weaned from their mother and running around, so probably from four weeks onwards. At six weeks, you will see the puppies play and they will start tugging at your shoelaces and your trouser legs! This can be the best time to choose a puppy.

A Boxer puppy should be alert and interested in what is going on around him. You will be looking for strong bone formation, which means chunky knuckles on their legs. Check that the eyes are clear, the coat should be shiny and there should be plenty of excess skin on a well-covered, chubby body. Ask the breeder when the puppies were last wormed. If has not been done, the puppies may have a dull coat and a pot-belly rather than an overall roundness that you would want to see on the puppies.

Hopefully you will find all the puppies in good health, so it then comes down to a matter of choice – if the breeder is able to give you a choice. Often you will find the breeder is keeping the best pup to show, and several may have been pre-ordered before the litter was born. Don't be put off by this, as good stock will always be in demand, but make sure that you are happy with the puppies you are choosing from. If you want a particular colour and that is not available, then be prepared to go to another breeder, or to wait for your chosen breeder to have a litter with a puppy to suit your preference.

MAKING THE CHOICE

How are you going to choose which puppy to have? Some people will say choose the one

46

This puppy has a dark mask on his face.

The preferred white marking for a show dog.

that comes and makes a fuss of you, but leave the retiring, quiet one who stays in the corner. While there can be some truth in this, it could just mean that the quiet puppy was tearing round before you arrived and is now tired. Another consideration is that the very lively puppy could end up being quite a handful as it grows up, and you will have to work harder on the training of this puppy.

The most likely scenario is that you will just find one puppy more appealing, or a pup may start licking you and tugging at your clothes, and you will just feel a stronger pull to one more

than the others. If you are looking for a pet, then this is fine and it is best to go with what your heart is telling you.

SHOW PUPPY

Looking for a show puppy is a completely different matter. You will need to do some research about the bloodlines you wish to buy from, and you will probably have visited many shows to see what attracts you to a dog in the ring. If you like a particular puppy, then find out who the parents are and contact their breeder to see if a litter is planned. It is much harder to buy a puppy for showing, as the

breeder will invariably keep the best prospect for themselves. However, there are often two or three in a litter that could be good show prospects with the right care and handling.

There are important aspects to look at when choosing a show puppy. If you are a complete novice, choose a well-respected breeder whose stock you have admired and arrange an appointment to visit. Tell the breeder that your knowledge is very limited and you are seeking their advice. You will find that most breeders value their reputation and will not sell you a puppy to show if they feel you will be wasting your time. A responsible breeder will advise you on what to look for, and how to rear your puppy to ensure that he stands the best chance in the show ring. It will then be up to you to put the time in at puppy training and ringcraft. It is important to read the Breed Standard and to fully understand it beforehand so that you have an idea of what you are looking for. For more information, see Chapter Seven: The Perfect Boxer.

When choosing a show puppy, the first thing you will look at will be the head. The skull should be domed, a bit like a policeman's helmet, with some wrinkles evident. The muzzle should be broad, giving a square appearance to the head. Some puppies will have a plain face, with a black mask all around the eyes, nose and mouth. However, the preferred look for showing is that there is a central panel of white markings between the eyes down to the top of the nose, and then running down either side of the muzzle to the upper lip. This gives a very attractive appearance.

The eyes must be dark; light or yellow eyes will be heavily penalised, as will one or both eyes having an unpigmented third eyelid. The eyes should not be too wide apart, as this will give a strange expression. The eyes should also be a nice almond shape, not too round or too slanted. The nose should be cold and wet and should be fully pigmented black.

If the puppies are old enough to be stood up, the breeder will be happy to show you what they look like. It will be quite hard at this stage to know exactly how the body will develop, as a lot of this depends on correct feeding and exercise. An excellent puppy prospect can end up with a weak back end due to lack of exercise and not being given the correct food to maintain healthy bone. Make sure you listen to the breeder's advice on this aspect of puppy rearing.

Once you are happy with the soundness of the puppy, you are probably ready to decide whether

It may suit your lifestyle to take on an older dog who needs rehoming.

you want to commit to buying this puppy or whether you want to look at other litters. The important consideration is to keep the breeder informed. If you have seen their litter and want to look at another before making a decision, give a timescale when you will get back to them. The breeder will probably tell you that if another purchaser comes along in the meantime, you may miss out, but if you are uncertain, then that will be a risk you will have to take. What is more likely is that you will decide you want that puppy there and then! If it is six weeks old, you will probably have to wait another two weeks before you can collect the puppy, but this gives you time to make sure that all is well at home and you are fully prepared for the new member of your family.

RESCUED/OLDER DOGS

You may decide you want a Boxer but do not want a puppy. If an adult would be better suited to your lifestyle, you have several options. The first is to contact breeders as you would for a puppy, but to explain that you would prefer an adult. It may happen that a breeder rears a dog for showing, but he has not made the grade for one reason or another and needs a new home.

In this situation, make sure you go to see the dog and ensure that you spend some time with him before agreeing to take him home. Watch out for signs of aggression, as you would not want to take on a dog with behavioural problems. Ask the breeder if there have been any health problems, so that you know exactly what you are taking on.

Another option is to take on a rescued dog. Unfortunately, too many Boxers these days end up in rescue, usually through no fault of their own. Most areas of the UK have a Boxer breed rescue and you can find these by contacting the Kennel Club or the breed club secretaries. There are other animal sanctuaries – such as the Blue Cross, Battersea Dogs Home, or Dogs Trust – that rehome dogs, but it may be harder to find a Boxer through these organisations.

Taking in a rescued Boxer can be very rewarding but can, occasionally, bring problems. Boxers are given up for rehoming for a number of reasons – elderly owners can no longer care for them, the owner has died, a new baby comes along... Some rescued dogs have health problems and some have behavioural problems that the owners cannot cope with. What is important for you is knowing exactly what the problems are, and whether they are issues you can deal with.

For example, if a Boxer has been the centre of the family for a young couple and they have treated him like a baby, he may well become jealous of the new baby, whom he feels is taking his place. The parents become protective of their child and do not realise that pushing the dog away is confusing and making him unhappy. In this instance, Boxer Rescue would look for a loving person or couple who are prepared to devote their time to the dog and his needs, whereas a house with children is unlikely to be the right environment for him.

Taking on a Boxer who has learned bad habits will require more care and attention than rearing a new puppy with no bad habits to unlearn. Aggression towards other dogs in the home or while exercising could be another reason for rehoming and will require the new owners to be firm but loving in retraining this Boxer.

Boxer Rescue or any animal rescue service will vet you and your home thoroughly before allowing you to see a dog they need to rehome. They have to be so careful in the selection process, as the worst thing for you and the dog is that it doesn't work out and the dog is returned to the kennels for further rehoming. This will take time and you must be patient during the vetting process. It will all be worthwhile in the end!

THE NEW ARRIVAL

Chapter 4

Once you have decided that a Boxer is the breed for you and your family, you will need to start preparing for the new puppy's arrival.

One of the top priorities is to provide a place that the puppy can call his own, a bed where he can go for 'time out' and peace and quiet, away from the hustle and bustle of family life. There are many types of bed on the pet market, from beanbags to plastic beds, which can be made cosy with a nice comfy blanket for your pup to snuggle in to. However, I have always found a crate very useful when you have a puppy, as you can have his bed at one end and newspaper at the other if the pup needs to relieve himself during the night. The crate can be left open during the day so the puppy can go in and out at will, but you can shut the

pup in for a nap or when he needs time out from the family.

A journey in the car will be much safer and less stressful if your Boxer travels in a crate. If you need to visit family and friends while your puppy is not completely house trained, or have to stay in a hotel, the crate will keep your puppy safe and out of mischief. You have the added bonus of knowing the puppy will be happy in his own space and will settle much better.

A crate is invaluable for a puppy, but most adult Boxers continue to use their doggy 'den'. For this reason, it is advisable to buy a crate that is big enough to use when your Boxer is fully grown. The size I recommend is 30 ins long, 25 ins wide, 27 high (76 x 63.5 x 69 cms). This allows the dog to stretch out flat on his side without being cramped up, and to sit up without hitting his head on the roof.

It is most important that your dog does not feel isolated in his crate, so it is a good idea to place it where most of the family congregates. Most people choose the kitchen, which is usually the hub of the house, or a corner of the lounge. A crate has the added bonus that the dog can see what is going on around him and doesn't feel left out. The mesh allows for free ventilation, and on colder evenings, a lightweight blanket can be draped over the top to prevent draughts.

CRATE TRAINING

When using a crate for the first time, make it as cosy as possible, lining it with a comfy blanket and maybe an old item of your own clothing that carries your scent, to give him comfort.

• Tempt your puppy into the crate with treats, so he associates going to bed with a

A Boxer who is trained to use a crate from an early age will look at it as his own special den.

good experience. Do this several times a day until he is happy to go into his crate.

- Shut the door for short periods of time, and sit next to him and comfort him if he cries.
- As soon as you feel confident that you can safely leave him alone, do so for short periods of half an hour to an hour.
- A puppy will settle better if he has something to do in the crate, so leave him a toy or a chew bone to occupy him.
- For reasons of safety, remove your puppy's collar when he is in the crate.

It may take a little while before your puppy settles in his crate, but be persistent; comfort him, but be firm, and he will soon

learn that it is a good place to be. It should be stressed that the puppy must never be shut in the crate for long periods of time, or as a punishment, as this is cruel, but when used sensibly, a crate is a godsend.

SAFETY IN THE GARDEN
Before you get your new puppy, you will need to ensure that your garden has dog-proof fencing so that he is secure at all times. Boxers are great jumpers, and even the smallest of bitches is capable of clearing a six-foot fence from a standstill. Having said that, Boxers love their families, and, as a breed, they do not generally tend to stray.

If you have a garden pond, it needs to be covered with a

suitable type of netting to prevent the curious puppy falling in and drowning. Likewise, if you are lucky enough to have a swimming pool, this should be covered or safely fenced off. Boxer puppies have no fear and are great investigators so will delight in exploring every nook and cranny.

Please ensure that you do not put down slug pellets – they are attractive to a dog and, if ingested, can prove fatal. There are also some plants that are poisonous to dogs, so you would be well advised to obtain more information about the plants that are in your garden to be sure you are not putting your puppy in any danger.

If you have some favourite plants, then I suggest you block them off from your new puppy, as he will delight in pulling off the flower heads and bringing them to you as a present. When he starts to teethe at about three months, he will become a great gardener, pruning bushes and plants alike, and digging holes in the lawn with great enthusiasm. It is often easier to fence off a small part of the garden for your puppy to call his own so he can play there safely, and use it as a toileting area. If you live in a flat, then you should provide your puppy with a play pen or similar enclosure where your puppy can let off a bit of steam.

BUYING EQUIPMENT
Dogs do not need a huge amount of equipment – a bed or a crate will be your biggest

investment – but there are a few essential items on the shopping list.

BEDDING

You will need a minimum of two pieces of bedding to allow for regular washing. Your Boxer will be perfectly happy with an old blanket, but the most convenient and hygienic bedding is synthetic fleece, which is specially made for dogs. This type of bedding is machine-washable and dries very quickly.

COLLAR AND LEAD

The puppy will need a collar and lead to fit him when you bring him home. It should be suitable for the size and weight of the puppy, and you will need to replace it as he grows. I use a soft, lightweight nylon collar and lead when the puppy is small. These are readily available in pet stores, and come in the most amazing variety of colours and patterns. As your puppy becomes accustomed to his collar and lead and gets stronger, you will find that a leather collar and lead is a sound investment, and will last a long while.

The Boxer has a very strong neck and chest, and many people opt for the various types of nylon or leather harnesses that are available. It is all a matter of personal choice, depending on how you and your dog adapt to the equipment. A full-grown adult can be very powerful and headstrong, so a headcollar or Halti may prove to be the best choice.

ID

The collar should have an identity tag with your address and telephone number on it. When your puppy comes home, it is a good idea to get him microchipped by your vet, as this provides a permanent record of ownership, should he ever get lost or stolen. His details will be held on a central registry, and can be checked by scanning him with a hand-held scanner. Tattooing is another method of identification; often breeders will get their whole litter tattooed before they go to their new homes.

BOWLS

There are many types of feeding bowls on the market, including plastic, ceramic and stainless steel. The cheapest is the plastic variety, but these can be chewed. My Boxers love to pick up their dishes and carry them around, so although a fancy ceramic dish looks very attractive, they have their limitations. I always use stainless-steel bowls; these are easy to keep clean and are virtually indestructible.

Your Boxer will need one bowl for food and another for fresh water, which should be available at all times. The water bowl should be of a generous size, as when a Boxer drinks, copious amounts escape from his jowls. If the bowl is too small, you will be left with large puddles around the bowl.

An inquisitive puppy will investigate anything and everything he comes across.

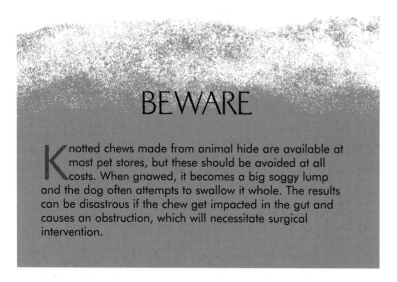

BEWARE

Knotted chews made from animal hide are available at most pet stores, but these should be avoided at all costs. When gnawed, it becomes a big soggy lump and the dog often attempts to swallow it whole. The results can be disastrous if the chew get impacted in the gut and causes an obstruction, which will necessitate surgical intervention.

Boxers love to play, so you will need to provide safe, suitable toys.

TOYS

You might want to buy your puppy a few toys so that he doesn't become bored. Initially, while he is quite small, he will get endless fun out of plastic flower pots, and items such as yoghurt cartons, egg boxes and cardboard boxes, which cost nothing and can easily be replaced when destroyed. A squeaky toy gives hours of fun, but it should be big enough so that it can't be swallowed. This type of toy should always be given under supervision in case the puppy manages to remove the squeaker and is in danger of choking on it. Squeaky toys always come out in the evening when you all settle down and are watching your favourite TV programme!

A new type of toy on the market, which gives endless hours of fun, is a rubber Kong. This has great entertainment value, as it is designed to be stuffed with your puppy's favourite food or treats.

BONES AND CHEWS

The butcher will supply you with a beef marrow bone, which will amuse your puppy when he is teething and he will appreciate a good chew. As an alternative, you can buy flavoured nylon chew bones, which do not splinter but massage the gums safely.

GROOMING KIT

The Boxer's coat is smooth and glossy so needs a minimum of attention. However, a weekly rub down with a rubber curry comb or glove will remove dead hairs and will keep the skin healthy.

You will also need to invest in a good pair of nail clippers in order to keep your Boxer's nails in trim. The best type to buy are the guillotine nail clippers, which are available from most pet shops. Although regular road walking should keep your dog's nails reasonably short, there are times when they grow too long and will need trimming. I hate to see a Boxer with long nails, as it completely spoils the appearance of the feet, and must be uncomfortable for the dog.

FINDING A VET

It is useful to make enquiries in order to find a veterinary practice before you actually get your puppy. Your breeder may like to advise you if you live in their area, but otherwise it is a good idea to ask local dog owners which veterinary surgery they use, and what they think of the service that is provided. You can look in the local Yellow Pages for a vet, too; you will also find veterinary hospitals advertised with 24-hour cover.

At last the big day arrives when it is time to collect your puppy.

When you do find a vet, ask what services are provided, particularly for out-of-hours and house calls. When things go wrong, they often do so at night, so you need the added assurance that help is readily available when you need it. If you are not happy with the first veterinary practice you find, look for another. A good vet, who knows your dog, is priceless – I have been with the same vet for over 30 years.

COLLECTING YOUR PUPPY

Puppies are usually ready to go to their new homes at around seven to eight weeks of age. It would be very unusual to collect a puppy any younger than seven weeks and, in my opinion, it is not desirable. If the litter is large, the breeder may want the puppies to stay for another week to ensure that they are fully independent of their dam.

Try to collect your puppy in the morning, as he will then have all day to get used to his new surroundings. It is a mistake to collect him in the evening, as he will soon be left alone in this strange, new, scary place when his owners retire for the night. When you collect your puppy, take a blanket or a towel for him to sit on and a supply of kitchen towels and a plastic bag in case he is travel sick. He will not be used to travelling in a car, and will probably be more comfortable on your knee, where you can talk to him and reassure him if he gets upset, rather than putting him in a crate or carrier, where he may become stressed.

HOME PACKAGE
The breeder will give you a copy of your puppy's pedigree, his Kennel Club registration papers (which the breeder will have signed, enabling you to then transfer change of ownership to

Arriving in a new home is a bewildering experience for a puppy.

arriving at his new home must be a real shock to the system. Boxer puppies soon acclimatise themselves, however, if a similar regime that he is used to is followed, and if everything is done to make his arrival a pleasant and comfortable experience.

VACCINATIONS

When you bring your puppy home, he will not have had any vaccinations, and therefore you should be extremely careful with him and not take him out in public places where unvaccinated dogs may roam, or allow him to come into contact with any strange dogs, as this would put him in serious danger.

Puppies are usually vaccinated in the UK against leptospirosis, hepatitis, parvovirus, distemper and hardpad. This usually takes the form of two injections two weeks apart, given at approximately eight weeks of age and 10 weeks of age, although this can vary slightly from vet to vet. This is a good time to introduce your new puppy to the vet and get him checked over, and also to discuss his future worming programme. Once your puppy has had his vaccinations, you can start taking him out. For more information on vaccinations, see Chapter 8: Happy and Healthy.

ARRIVING HOME

When you arrive home with your new puppy, it is a very exciting time for all the family, especially the children. However, it is

yourself), a receipt for the full purchase price, and a worming certificate that tells you when your puppy was last wormed and what drug was used. We always worm our puppies at three, five and seven weeks of age, and recommend that the new owner seeks veterinary advice as to the date of the next worming. We also supply six weeks' free insurance cover from the time that the puppy leaves us, with the option for the new owners to take out a policy with the

company when the six weeks is up. We feel that this gives the new puppy owner peace of mind.

The breeder will also supply you with a full diet sheet and a supply of the food that the puppy is used to. Going to a new home is a traumatic time for a puppy. He will be leaving his littermates whom he has come to rely on both for confidence and company. He will have never been alone, and will have become acclimatised and familiar with his surroundings and routine, so

important to resist the temptation of asking all your friends and neighbours round to view your new addition, as it will be all too much for him

The best plan is to let the puppy explore his new surroundings, under your watchful eye, to ensure he doesn't get into trouble. If you have children, please ensure that there are no small toys lying around that can be chewed or, worse, swallowed. When the puppy is tired, he must be allowed to go to his bed and sleep. A young puppy needs plenty of rest in order to grow and thrive. Boxer puppies are very resilient and keep going, no matter how tired they are. Learn to recognise the signs that your puppy needs to rest and put him in his bed or crate and allow him to sleep.

MEETING THE FAMILY

I am often asked whether Boxers are good with children and my reply is: "Yes, they are, but are your children good with dogs?" The Boxer will thrive on the closeness of a family with children that treat him with love and respect, and he, in turn, will return that love a hundredfold.

When a new puppy arrives home, the children will be hugely excited, but they must learn that the puppy is not a plaything, and his needs must be respected. Small puppies need a lot of rest. To begin with, a puppy will have a short burst of play followed by a sleep. He will also have a long sleep after a meal.

It should be obvious when your puppy is tired – he will keep flopping on the floor, only to get up and start playing again. When this happens, be firm – put the puppy in a quiet place, such as his crate, and let him sleep. You will need to explain to children that the puppy needs his rest. Puppies grow when they are asleep, and they will also become fractious and irritable if they are overtired.

If you have young children, do not allow them to pick up the puppy. Puppies do not stay still for long, and a pup can wriggle free and fall, sometimes with disastrous consequences. The best plan is to make sure the child is sitting on the floor before allowing the puppy to be held and cuddled.

THE RESIDENT DOG

If you already have another dog, introduce the new puppy tactfully to ensure that their relationship gets off to a good start. When the two dogs first

Try not to interfere as the puppy and resident dog get to know each other – they will soon sort out their relationship.

takes on a new lease of life with his new companion.

BEDTIME

You need to decide where your puppy is going to sleep – and stick to it. The first night away from his dam and siblings is going to be difficult, so it is important to make certain preparations to reduce the stress that he may feel. He will be used to snuggling up with his littermates for comfort and warmth during the night, so make his bed comfortable with a soft blanket and maybe a cuddly toy to snuggle up to. If it is winter, wrap a hot-water bottle in a towel for warmth. It is said that the ticking of an alarm clock, wrapped up in a towel, imitates the beating of his littermates' hearts and is comforting – certainly it can do no harm.

You will need to be firm with your puppy, and if he cries, reassure him and put him back into his bed. He will soon become used to his new routine. That said, I usually end up putting the new puppy's bed next to my own for the first few days so that when he wakes in the night and cries, a hand gently stroking him provides the reassurance that he is not alone and he usually goes straight back to sleep. Once he is more confident and settled in his new surroundings, I move his bed to the kitchen, which will be his permanent bedroom. What works for me may not work for you – it is all a matter of trial and error.

On the first night your puppy will miss the comfort of snuggling up with his littermates.

meet, it is wise to keep the pup on your lap while allowing the older dog to sniff him and get acquainted. The older dog may growl, and the puppy may be rather boisterous at first. Stroke your older dog to reassure him that he is your favourite! When the two dogs meet on ground level, it is best to go into the garden, where the older dog will feel less protective, and you can keep a watchful eye on proceedings.

One of my older dogs tends to stand over a new puppy and follow him everywhere. But even if the resident dog appears welcoming, he may not be happy to share his bed or food bowls with the new arrival. The puppy may try to creep into bed with

the older dog (who may growl) and then get up to go and lie down elsewhere. This may go on for a few days.

Initially, feed the dogs separately to avoid any confrontation over food, and, in the first week, do not leave the two dogs together unsupervised at any time. The situation must be carefully monitored as they get to know each other. If the puppy is annoying the older dog, try to distract him with a toy. Give the older dog lots of praise, and make sure you always fuss him first, before paying attention to the puppy, to reinforce pack leadership.

I have found that even the most grumpy old dog will accept a puppy, and the oldie often

FEEDING A BOXER PUPPY

For the first few days at least, it is wise not to change your puppy's food and, if at all possible, try to keep to the same feeding routines that he has become used to. Initially your puppy may only pick at his food due to the change of home and all the new things that he has to get used to, but this will soon pass once he has settled. Do not leave his food down too long, and, once he has eaten what he wants, take it up and do not offer any food until the next mealtime. This will encourage the pup to clean up his meals quickly – there is nothing worse than a fussy feeder.

The breeder will have given you a comprehensive diet sheet and a supply of the food that your puppy has been raised on. Try to stick to this for at least a week before you make any changes at all. If you wish to change your puppy's diet for whatever reason, it is best to wait until he has settled into his new home before making any dietary changes. It makes sense that if you want to change the puppy's food then it should be replaced with a food of similar good quality that will keep the puppy well covered and produce nice round bone. There are no short cuts here, so do not be tempted to buy the cheapest food possible. There are many good-quality foods on the market to choose from and once you find one that suits your puppy, it is best to stick to it. Too many changes are not good for a puppy, so take things slowly.

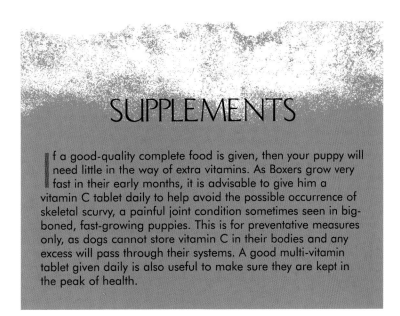

SUPPLEMENTS

If a good-quality complete food is given, then your puppy will need little in the way of extra vitamins. As Boxers grow very fast in their early months, it is advisable to give him a vitamin C tablet daily to help avoid the possible occurrence of skeletal scurvy, a painful joint condition sometimes seen in big-boned, fast-growing puppies. This is for preventative measures only, as dogs cannot store vitamin C in their bodies and any excess will pass through their systems. A good multi-vitamin tablet given daily is also useful to make sure they are kept in the peak of health.

QUANTITY

Always feed according to appetite; it is my firm belief that you cannot give a growing puppy too much food. If he clears his dish quickly, then increase the quantity gradually until he is satisfied. You will only get out of your puppy what you put into him. I would much prefer my puppy to have a good covering over his bones than have him skinny. If he contracts any illness and goes off his food for a couple of days, a layer of fat will stand him in good stead and he will not lose too much condition. Occasionally, puppies get upset tummies and it's best to miss a couple of meals to give the stomach a rest, then perhaps give him a dish of natural yoghurt, which they love. For more information on feeding, see Chapter 5: The Best of Care.

WATER

Last but not least, make sure that fresh water is available at all times. This water should be changed several times a day, as Boxers are the messiest drinkers around. They have a trick of storing water in their jowls and dribbling over the surrounding area, delighting in wiping it on the nearest available knee or soft furnishings.

TOILET TRAINING

When you get your puppy home, take him out to the chosen spot in the garden and ask him to be clean. You should always use the same place and he will associate this place with being clean. Use the same command each time, too, such as "Be clean," and wait until he performs. Be lavish with your praise and he will soon get the hang of things.

If you take your puppy into the garden at regular intervals, he will soon understand what is required.

here, and will pay dividends in the long run. In between times, try to put your puppy out on the hour, or at least at regular short intervals. This is time-consuming at first, but he will soon get the idea. Boxer puppies are naturally clean, and as soon as they are on their legs they will crawl off their bed to be clean on the newspaper.

It takes a small puppy a little while to be clean at night. If you are using a crate, line the front with newspaper and the puppy will quickly learn to use this rather than soil his bedding. If your pup is not in a crate, surround the bed with newspaper and spread some at the back door to give him the idea that he is to go outside to be clean. Once the puppy gets the hang of it, you can reduce the area of newspaper that you are providing and then gradually remove it altogether.

Remember to ignore any accidents that your puppy might have. Never scold him for his mistakes, as he will not associate them with your anger; rather he will learn to become afraid of you.

It must be said that summer puppies are easier to train, because if the weather is fine, you can leave the back door open and the puppy is free to come and go as he pleases. In the winter, when it is cold and raining, then house training becomes more of a chore, as the garden is not such an attractive place for either owner or puppy, and training may take just that little bit longer

Your puppy will want to 'go' immediately after he wakes up, after he has eaten, and following a play session. Learn to watch for the telltale signs of rushing around in circles and sniffing the ground. The instant you see this behaviour, pick your puppy up, take him to his chosen spot and wait for a result.

If he doesn't immediately go to the toilet, do not take him back indoors, as he will probably go when he gets back inside. Be patient. Outside is a whole new world, and a pup may initially forget the reason why he was put there as he rushes off to investigate new and exciting things. Consistency is the key

 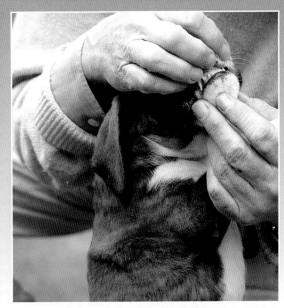

Accustom your puppy to being handled, and then he will not struggle when he has to see the vet.

HANDLING

From the outset, your puppy will be picked up and fussed and cuddled, which he will, no doubt, enjoy, and this can also provide a good opportunity to give him a quick check over.

- A Boxer puppy's coat should be tight and glossy, and should be checked for fleas or any other parasites that he could pick up (see Chapter Eight: Happy and Healthy).
- Examine the ears to check that they are clean, pink and healthy. Any debris should be removed with a piece of damp cotton wool. I make a point of wiping out a puppy's ears on a weekly basis, whether it is needed or not, so that the pup becomes accustomed to the routine and accepts it in a calm manner. This is invaluable, because if there is any signs of redness in the ears or a smelly discharge, then a trip to the vet will be necessary and it will make the vet's job so much easier if the pair of you don't have to put the puppy into a stranglehold to be examined!
- Check the nails, as they grow very fast and may need trimming. I use guillotine clippers, and just remove the little hook that forms on the end of the nail. It is essential that your puppy allows you to trim his nails, so be firm from the outset, and give lots of praise when the job is done.

HOUSE RULES

It is most important to establish house rules as soon as your puppy arrives in his new home. It seems so cute to have your puppy on the furniture with you, but maybe not so pleasant when he is fully grown and weighs around five-plus stones (32 kgs)!

If you do not intend to allow your puppy on the furniture, be firm, and put him on his blanket, or sit him on the floor, giving him a cuddle so that he knows you still love him! The same rules apply when you decide where your puppy will sleep at night, and what areas of the house and garden he is allowed to use. Consistency is the key; it is important that the whole family adhere to the rules, and your

A puppy will get as much exercise as he needs from playing in the garden.

puppy will soon get the message.

EXERCISING YOUR PUPPY

Initially your puppy will get all the exercise he needs in your garden. You will find that as he grows, his rest periods become shorter and his playtimes longer.

You can give your puppy short lead walks to socialise him and to introduce him to all the new sights and sounds of the outside world. It is often a good idea to take him on the school run or to walk outside a school in the morning or at home time, where he will encounter many new sights and sounds. Everyone loves a puppy, so you may find that you are constantly stopped while your puppy is fussed. This is very good for him and teaches him to be sociable.

At this stage, a Boxer puppy does not need 10-mile hikes and long, boisterous games of football with the children (although he will revel in these when an adult!). Too much exercise puts undue strain on the joints, and your Boxer may not grow to his full potential. By the time your Boxer is 12 months of age, he will have done most of his growing and his exercise can be more rigorous.

TAKING ON AN OLDER DOG

If you have decided to take on an adult Boxer, you will need to spend time settling him into your home. You may have by-passed the rather messy and troublesome puppy stage, but an adult may also have special needs.

Try to find out as much as you can about your new Boxer's background. Obviously you will have established whether he is good with children, and is happy to live with other dogs, cats, or small animals before making your choice, but there is other information which can be helpful. If possible, find out the type of food he is used to, if he is accustomed to sleeping in a crate, and if he has any particular likes or dislikes. The

Establish a regular routine to help an older dog settle into his new home.

aim is to make the transition into a new home as easy as possible, and this attention to detail will help your Boxer to settle more quickly.

When he first arrives home, treat him in just the same way as you would a puppy, taking him out to the garden, showing him his sleeping quarters, and introducing him to members of the family. For the first few weeks, try to keep life at a low-key level so that your Boxer can get used to his new surroundings with the minimum of stress.

As with a puppy, resist the temptation of inviting friends and neighbours round until the dog has settled. It is important that your Boxer has a chance to get to know his new family first.

Generally, an older dog will settle reasonably quickly, as long as you introduce a structured routine, and treat him with kindness and patience, in just the same way as taking a new puppy into your home.

THE BEST OF CARE

Chapter 5

We all learn from our experiences, dealing with different circumstances, and sometimes we learn the hard way. So if you take some good advice at an early stage, it will get you all off to the best start: you, your family and, of course, your Boxer! I will endeavour to give you, the reader, a good, all-round, balanced approach as to what the Boxer needs.

The Boxer is a great family dog, but he needs good management from all angles from an early age. He needs a safe environment, food and water, exercise, education and lots of love and attention – but always remember that he is a dog and should know the house rules and his place within the family, which is his 'pack'.

In this chapter I will cover feeding, grooming and exercise. I will start with the food and nutritional needs of the Boxer; I find the best approach here is to try to keep the diet simple. There are so many choices on the market today, with so many food producers who are all trying to make their mark – so where to start?

FOOD REQUIREMENTS
There are two main categories of food, which are needed in the diet:

- **Protein:** This is used to build body tissues and is found in meat, chicken and fish.
- **Carbohydrates:** These provide the body with energy and are found in biscuit, pasta, potatoes and rice.

Animal fat is also important as an energy source and it contains some essential vitamins. It also can give texture and flavour to food. The dog needs a number of vitamins and minerals, mainly vitamin A, B and C, as we do, and calcium is needed during early growth and to maintain healthy teeth and bones.

Dogs are designed to cope with a meat diet; their teeth are made to tear meat into chunks, not to grind it down like the horse. In the wild, dogs would have eaten the whole of an animal, so an expensive lean meat diet will not provide all the food requirements. In Britain it is possible to buy blocks of deep-frozen dog food – tripe, tripe and beef, tripe and chicken, etc, which Boxers love. The disadvantage is that it needs slow defrosting, and it can have a disagreeable smell, which, in turn, passes through the dog! There are many theories regarding feeding; I shall not attempt to cover them all or to

The Boxer needs a well-balanced diet that is suited to his age and lifestyle.

advise the right diet for you and your Boxer. However, I shall give you some of the options, which, with the help of your puppy's breeder, will help you to decide which is the most suitable. A puppy's health and growing needs are the most important factors, but we must also consider breed-specific issues. These include protein requirements for the Boxer, which is a very lively, active dog, the condition and sensitivity of his skin and stomach, and the calcium needed for good bone growth in a large breed.

BARF DIETS

I would just like to touch on the BARF (Biologically Appropriate Raw Food) diet, which aims to maximise the health reproduction capacity of the animal, and, by doing so, minimises the need for veterinary intervention. Basically, it means that you feed the animal the diet it evolved to eat. These are the methods commonly used and endorsed by zoos and those concerned with preserving endangered species. However, the BARF diet is not endorsed by major food companies, and many vets are opposed to it.

The diet must contain the same balance and type of ingredient as those eaten by dogs' wild ancestors, including muscle meat, bone, fat, organ meat, and vegetable materials. This type of food may not be readily available, convenient, or pleasant to prepare. However, significant research has been conducted showing positive benefits, and for

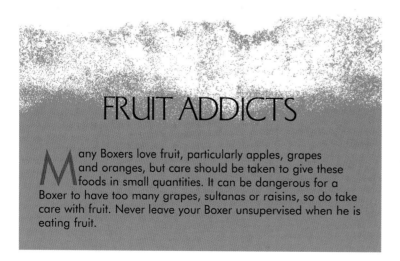

FRUIT ADDICTS

Many Boxers love fruit, particularly apples, grapes and oranges, but care should be taken to give these foods in small quantities. It can be dangerous for a Boxer to have too many grapes, sultanas or raisins, so do take care with fruit. Never leave your Boxer unsupervised when he is eating fruit.

A complete diet is specially formulated to meet a dog's nutritional needs.

Canned food can be fed as a complete meal mixed with biscuit, or some Boxer owners use canned food to add flavour to a complete diet.

those of you who are already 'organic', it may be just what you are looking for. As long as the dog's all-round diet is balanced, there should be no harm done. I have not had any experience of this diet, but feel it does deserve a mention. More information can be found on numerous websites.

MODERN COMPLETE DIETS

Complete diets are the most commonly used because they are so convenient. The plus points include the following:
• Complete diets are specially manufactured to provide all the goodness that a dog needs.
• They are easily available.
• They come in a huge variety of flavours.
• They are tailored to meet specific needs and life stages.

Cost does vary, but do not be fooled into thinking that the more you pay, the better the food will be, as this is not necessarily

the case. Manufacturers of complete foods spend many thousands of pounds on marketing, packaging and research, which may be reflected in the cost. The most important consideration for you, as an owner, is that you are satisfied that you are providing your Boxer with what he needs.

When choosing a diet, use a reputable brand and read the label to check the protein levels. I would recommend the lower protein scores for a Boxer. Some of the cheaper brands do include all the necessary dietary needs, but with my young stock I am particularly careful that they get good quality.

Complete foods mainly come as dry food, called kibble; this will vary in size dependant on the size of animal, age, working needs etc. Complete wet food can be bought in tins and foil trays. The flavouring is important, as we want our

Boxers to like their food, but this should not be the most important factor. Consider also the effects the food will have. For example, an all-tinned, soft-food diet is not best for the condition of teeth, as we know a dog's teeth were made to tear and chew and bite. A dog should, therefore, have some foodstuffs that enable this to happen.

Most of us like to feed a combination of a complete diet with the addition of canned food, meat or fish to provide some variety. It is important to bear in mind that the complete diet provides the bulk of the meal; the additional food gives added taste and texture. The manufacturers of complete diets recommend that no supplements are added, but many owners and breeders have found the combined system meets the specific needs of the Boxer.

Whatever method of feeding you choose to adopt, keep it

BONE OF CONTENTION

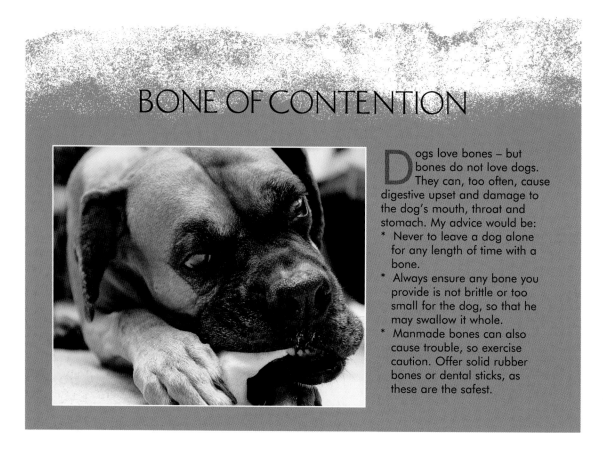

Dogs love bones – but bones do not love dogs. They can, too often, cause digestive upset and damage to the dog's mouth, throat and stomach. My advice would be:

* Never to leave a dog alone for any length of time with a bone.
* Always ensure any bone you provide is not brittle or too small for the dog, so that he may swallow it whole.
* Manmade bones can also cause trouble, so exercise caution. Offer solid rubber bones or dental sticks, as these are the safest.

simple. Don't make life hard for yourself by giving your dog too much choice and a different flavour every night – you could make the puppy very fussy and this will continue throughout his life. By keeping the diet simple, life will be easier in the longer term. Convenience is also a factor that needs to be considered, and a more natural home-cooked diet, such as the BARF diet, will take a lot more time to prepare than a complete dog food bought from the supermarket!

FEEDING A BOXER PUPPY

When you have bought a new puppy, it is essential that you have detailed information from the breeder regarding all aspects of the puppy's early life, but especially his feeding regime. Speaking as a breeder, I always give new owners a detailed guide to what food the puppy has been fed, the quantity, the number of meals per day, as well as some dietary alternatives.

You will probably collect your puppy at eight weeks of age. At this stage, he will need to be fed

four or five times a day. This is reduced to four meals, and, by the time puppy is six months old, he will need two or three meals per day. I prefer to feed all my adult dogs at least twice a day, morning and evening. However, some owners feed just once a day and this can also work well. What is important is that the puppy/dog has a regular routine that fits well with your own family routine.

The best plan is to start by feeding the same diet as the breeder has chosen. A good

SAMPLE PUPPY DIET

Measuring cups are easily available from pet stores or from your vet.

BREAKFAST
Between a third to a quarter of a measuring scoop (50/80g) of complete puppy kibble (weaning puppy/puppy junior) moistened with hot water and allowed to cool. Mix with meat, chicken or fish, tinned or fresh (50/60g up to 100g) to add taste.

The amount needs to be increased as the puppy grows to half a scoop of complete kibble (150-200g) mixed with meat and then to a full scoop (75g approx) by six months old.

LUNCH
Two eggs scrambled, with some goats' milk which puppies find easier to digest. If you cannot get goats' milk, try semi-skimmed.

Some moistened kibble can also be added to this meal, as can grated cheese.

DINNER
Complete kibble plus meat as for breakfast.

SUPPER
The puppy will appreciate a warm milky supper; porridge or rice pudding usually goes down well. This can be substituted for breakfast or lunch to give variation.

Any of these meals can be supplemented by pasta, boiled potatoes or rice to aid weight gain and for variety. However, if puppy is already well covered, this may not be necessary. A gravy can also be added to help appetite/flavour.

breeder will be happy to share their knowledge and experience with you, and will probably give you some food to take home as a start. The puppy will be subject to many changes in the first few weeks away from his littermates, and may not eat well at all for the first few days. This is quite normal and as long as your puppy is drinking and seems healthy and lively, don't panic.

A growing puppy needs the right mix of protein and carbohydrates, plus sufficient vitamins and minerals. This is

Your Boxer puppy will need four meals a day when he arrives in his new home.

Make sure that fresh drinking water is always available.

when a complete puppy food is at its best. Be sure that it is specially designed with all the necessary ingredients for a puppy, as adult dog food will not provide sufficient levels of ingredients to enable healthy growth. Remember, too, that the puppy is constantly growing, so his needs and the amounts fed to him will change.

CHANGING DIET
Wherever possible, continue with what the breeder has been feeding. However, there may be good reasons to change from the breeder's diet, such as availability, cost, or if the puppy is not thriving. If you need to change the diet, do this over a period of at least a week to 10 days, gradually reducing the old and mixing/replacing it with the new food.

IMPORTANCE OF WATER
Your puppy should have access to fresh, clean water at all times. But it is also important that a puppy does not drink a whole bowl in one go, as this may cause sickness, a type of colic, stomach ache or, at worst, a twisted gut (gastric torsion). This can happen if a puppy eats quickly and then runs around, so it is a good idea to encourage rest after eating. Monitoring water intake is a daily task. Once you get to know the puppy, you will soon learn how much is normal for him and will notice when he either does not drink or drinks excessively – both of which can be signs of ill health. It is advisable to have the water in the same container/bowl and in the same place so that puppy can become accustomed to its place and will know where to find it. An adult dog will also

prefer to have his water conveniently placed so he always knows where it is.

Remember that if a dog is healthy and hungry, he will eat and drink. If he is healthy but not hungry, he will not eat. But if he is not eating, and appears disinterested, and is not drinking either, this could be a sign of ill health and your Boxer should be seen by a vet.

OBESITY IN BOXERS
Overfeeding a Boxer is an easy trap to fall into. Most Boxers love their food and will eat most things, so, as with young children, you need to be responsible for their diet and give them the best possible start in life.

Do not feed them titbits from the table, as this encourages bad behaviour and can induce

A Boxer should be lean and muscular, and carry no excess weight.

drooling. Chocolate is also an absolute no-no and can be dangerous to a Boxer, particularly if given in large quantities. A Boxer who steals a box of chocolates can become seriously ill or even die.

Obesity in dogs is common and will lead to additional health problems. The Boxer's heart will be under additional strain as well as all the other vital organs if he becomes obese, and this will also limit his ability to exercise properly.

We encourage new owners to give puppies access to food throughout the day in the first couple of months, but if a puppy becomes overweight at an early age, this will affect his ability to grow, and his bones and muscles will not grow in the correct proportions. A poor diet will also affect the dog's skin. It is important to weigh your puppy regularly – for example, each time he is wormed – and your vet will also be able to advise you on the

correct weight for your Boxer.

I don't want to generalise about a puppy's weight, as within the breed there can be vast differences in size, muscle tone and bone. If a bitch has been spayed, where she has been relieved of the stress of hormonal swings, then there may be an added tendency to weight gain. This needs to be monitored, and the diet reduced and exercise increased where necessary, to prevent obesity.

FEEDING INTO ADULTHOOD

A Boxer remains a puppy for a very long time in his head, although in terms of feeding, after about a year it is time to think of an adult diet. If you feed a complete diet, this would usually mean moving up to a maintenance food of the same brand and adjusting amounts accordingly. The adult dog also needs less protein and carbohydrate foods and will thrive on a steady diet of the same kibble and mixer meat each day.

I maintain that if the kibble is a complete food and keeps your Boxer in top condition, the mixer food does not have to be such high quality; it simply provides moisture, texture and taste. I have used tripe, tinned meat and chicken in the main – all of which are easily digested. In the UK, if a puppy's stools become loose, we use a brand that has a high cereal content, which helps to maintain good stool substance and is gentle for the puppy's stomach as it develops.

If your Boxer is unwell, pregnant, feeding pups or recovering from an operation or illness, a temporary change of diet may be necessary, but the usual diet should be resumed as soon as possible.

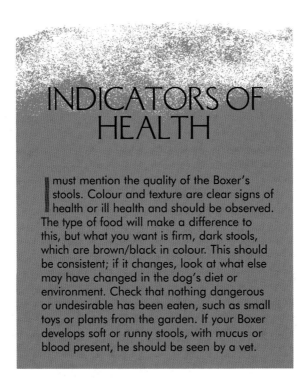

INDICATORS OF HEALTH

I must mention the quality of the Boxer's stools. Colour and texture are clear signs of health or ill health and should be observed. The type of food will make a difference to this, but what you want is firm, dark stools, which are brown/black in colour. This should be consistent; if it changes, look at what else may have changed in the dog's diet or environment. Check that nothing dangerous or undesirable has been eaten, such as small toys or plants from the garden. If your Boxer develops soft or runny stools, with mucus or blood present, he should be seen by a vet.

SAMPLE ADULT DIET

- **Breakfast:** Scoop of moistened kibble (150/175g) and about half a pound (200g) of mixer/meat.
- **Dinner:** As above.

I prefer to feed twice a day, as I just feel that once a day leaves an awfully long time in between feeds – but this is a matter of personal choice.

Please do not feel that the adult dog needs more variety, or needs to eat what you eat. What he needs is a balanced diet that meets his needs. Too much access to human food is not good for him, particularly as this often means high fat content. How well his diet

is working can be judged on the energy levels of the dog, his general condition, coat and skin condition, his appetite and his stools.

If all is well, then be happy to leave the diet alone – but, of course, they get treats! We always share our Christmas roast with the dogs! Treats for my own dogs consist of cheese, cooked sausage, corned beef, tuna, plus dental chews and biscuits.

If you are taking on a Boxer who is middle-aged – over two years of age and under seven – you may need to adjust the diet. Try to find out what the dog has been fed, and gradually make any changes over a week to 10 days. Always ask if there is a history of sensitivity to any foods or substances, so that difficulties and upsets may be avoided.

Once the Boxer becomes a veteran (over seven years officially), you may see a decline in his exercise needs, although to keep a healthy mind it is important to keep the dog active and challenged. Do not feel that exercise must be reduced; as long as the dog is willing and able, continue to exercise as usual, but eventually he will slow down and then you should consider a senior diet, which has reduced protein and provides additional vitamins to ease the journey into old age. Smaller meals, more often, may also be required.

FAST FOOD

Boxers are prone to eating rather too quickly, as they enjoy their food so much. This can lead to stomach upset, flatulence, and, in the worst case, a twisted gut. As Boxers eat quickly, they swallow a lot of air as they gulp down the food. They do not chew their food well and therefore digestion begins once the food reaches the stomach.

To ease digestion, ensure that the food you give does not have large lumps in it and is well chopped up. Never give your dog spiced food or leftover takeaway.

Boxers do have a tendency to eat grass and will graze contentedly on fresh growth. However, this may be a sign of an upset and the Boxer is trying to make himself sick to get rid of what is making his stomach uncomfortable. Always keep an eye on grazing and if the dog is eating grass to make himself sick, it may be worth a visit to the vet. With a regular sensible diet, adjusted throughout his growth from puppy to adult, your Boxer should remain in good health throughout his life.

Nutritional needs will change as a Boxer grows older.

GROOMING

All dogs of all ages need grooming regularly, and, as with children and horses, it is important to use this as an opportunity to check your Boxer's health.

Grooming should be an enjoyable task for both you and your dog, so teach your puppy to enjoy the attention – but also to behave. When you need to handle him, to check his ears and feet, the puppy must allow this and be patient. Puppies must be socialised and this includes going to the vet and allowing a hands-on examination by the vet.

NAILS

Clipping nails is a job that many owners back away from. Puppies should have had their claws clipped by the breeder at four, six and eight weeks, and then by new owners every few months if necessary. If nails are allowed to grow too long, they can interfere with correct movement. Puppies' feet should be cat-like with tight claws.

As with your own nails, you should see where the quick is. This is the pink inside of the nail (except with black nails where it cannot be seen!). If you learn to clip the very end of the nails, there is no danger of cutting into the quick. However, if you are worried about this task, ask an experienced dog owner or a

GROOMING KIT

You need a small grooming kit for your Boxer, which should include the following:
- A towel
- A soft brush for the coat
- A harder pad or hand glove to remove excess hair
- Nail clippers
- Small scissors
- A cloth or brush to polish the coat.

veterinary nurse to show you what to do.

EARS

A Boxer in the UK will have ears that fold over, but they fly back when he is running, which can mean that dirt that gets in often cannot get out. It is therefore important to check regularly for any debris. Lift up the ear and look deep inside; the ear should be pinkish, not red, and clean with no wax or brown dirt. Look out for mites – these will need treatment from a vet.

The Boxer's ear is an L shape, which makes it very difficult for your finger to damage the ear drum and therefore the inside of the ear is quite easy to clean. Fragrance-free baby wipes or special animal wipes can be used to keep the ear clean. If your

Boxer is shaking his head excessively, and/or rubbing his ear cheek, seek veterinary attention.

EYES

Boxers are prone to eye ulcers, which can be very slow to heal. If an ulcer is not treated correctly early on, it can lead to the loss of an eye. Always watch for any unusual changes in the eye, or uncharacteristic behaviour. Early signs would be red/blue colouring, closing the eye, the eye watering and excessive rubbing. Veterinary attention should be sought without delay.

Because of the shape of the Boxer's head, the wrinkles beneath their eyes can get sore and discoloured from tear staining, so check regularly and wipe clean any excess moisture. A little Vaseline in this area can help with soreness by protecting the skin from the moisture. If the area becomes very inflamed and sore, seek veterinary advice.

TEETH

The Boxer's jaw should be slightly undershot, which means that the top teeth should sit behind the bottom teeth. The jaw should be quite wide and straight with four large canine teeth – two on the upper jaw, and two on the lower jaw. The teeth should be white with pale pink gums; a

Nails will need trimming on a regular basis.

Wipes can be used to keep the ears fresh and clean.

good diet and jaw exercising (chewing/biting) will help with this. Look out for signs of tartar build-up – yellow/grey discolouring – and try to keep this to a minimum.

It is common practice to clean the teeth, using a brush and specially formulated toothpaste, which does help with dental health. Some owners opt for a scale and polish, which is carried out by a vet under general anaesthetic. If teeth get diseased and infected, they can be removed by a vet, although, again, this must be done under a general anaesthetic. Surprisingly, a dog can continue to do well after numerous extractions.

COAT CARE
The Boxer has a short coat, which makes grooming an easy job. The coat should be groomed with a grooming glove/mitt or soft brush daily, or at least every week. This will help to keep it free of dust and dirt, and allow you to check for fleas and ticks (see Chapter Eight: Happy and Healthy). I also use this opportunity to check other health issues, such as lumps and

bumps or any sign of soreness.

The dog should be brushed as a horse, the brush following the lie of the hair, from head to toe. Reasonably vigorous brushing will bring out the shine in the coat and help to tone muscles. The dog has natural oils in his coat, and these produce the shine, aided by a healthy diet.

The Boxer has folds running over the root of his nose, and these folds need to be kept sweet and clean. Use a soft, damp cloth to clean these folds on a daily basis, especially under the eyes, which can get sore.

COAT CARE

The Boxer has a low-maintenance coat and minimum effort is needed to keep it in good order.

Always brush with the lay of the coat.

Brushing has a massaging effect and also brings out the shine in the coat.

Use wipes over the body to clean and freshen the coat.

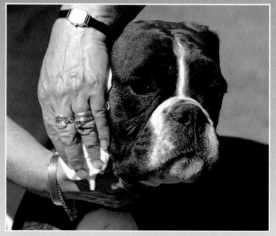

Clean between the creases on your Boxer's face to remove any debris.

SHOW PRESENTATION

If you are showing your Boxer, you will need to use
clippers to enhance his clean, muscular lines.

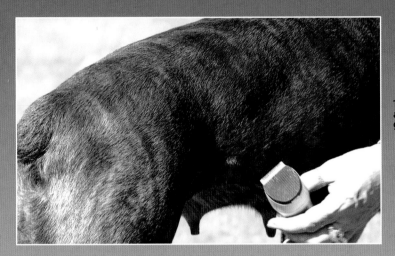

The clippers will trim the hairs
along the line of the body to
give a smooth outline.

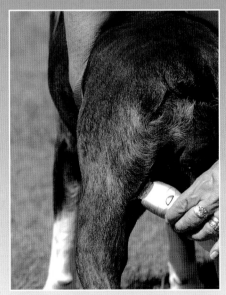

Trim the hindlegs, and, if docked, around the
tail.

Finish off by trimming the whiskers to give
the Boxer a typical clean, strong look.

FUN AND EXERCISE

The Boxer is a very physical dog and thrives on a variety of play and exercise.

A Boxer will need free-running exercise on a daily basis.

If a Boxer is playing, he is using both mind and body.

BATHING

Boxers don't really need to be bathed very often – no more than three or four times a year, unless your dog gets particularly muddy or falls in the canal! Make sure that you bath your dog in a safe environment – he may very well jump out at any time! I would recommend that a solid collar is worn, so the dog can be held firmly.

Do not use highly perfumed shampoos; try to keep to something natural. Always dry the dog off as thoroughly as possible, and allow him to stay in a warm place until he is absolutely dry.

The most fun place is in the garden in the summer – the Boxer just adores playing under a hose and drying out while basking in the sun!

EXERCISING YOUR BOXER

When your Boxer puppy is under six months, exercise should be limited (see Chapter Four: The New Arrival). But from six months onwards, he should be getting a good run at least once a day. He will need access to a garden, or a large indoor space where he is able to move around, such as a kitchen, conservatory or garage. If space is limited, then

more walks will need to be provided. I have always maintained that careful exercise (i.e. no stairs or excess jumping in the early years) will help in the long run.

A Boxer needs a variety of exercise, so give plenty of off-lead walks in the woods or park, and regular lead walking and socialising to keep him educated, challenged and ultimately a happy dog. If you have two or more dogs, they will play happily for hours, providing a great source of exercise. If you only have one dog, he may need additional walks to keep him in shape.

When you have the opportunity, meet up with friends who have dogs to make your walks more fun.

THE OLDER BOXER

So when does a Boxer become an old dog? The honest answer is that it can be anytime, dependent on the breeding, and the general health and life experiences of the dog. Dogs officially become 'older' when they reach the age of seven, when they are then referred to as a 'veteran'. However, my oldest Boxer is now 11 and she still races around with the others – she has the same lifestyle as the younger dogs, the same exercise and feeding regime. She still loves to play with a ball and gives all her grandchildren a good run for their money!

DIET AND EXERCISE

Once a Boxer is six to eight years of age, you should begin to review his needs, particularly his diet and exercise. The Boxer is certainly a breed where a careful upbringing – watching the weight, keeping to a steady reliable diet, and providing sufficient exercise – will pay dividends in later life.

A couch potato Boxer who is overweight and lazy will surely struggle in later life. An overweight dog cannot exercise properly, and he will be putting extra strain on the heart and, indeed, all the organs. Too much fat in the body may result in fatty cysts, eye ulcers and skin problems.

Once a Boxer has left the puppy stage of his life, at about a year old, the diet should be steady and consistent for a number of years. My 11-year-old has a little less now than the other dogs, but essentially she has the same food, twice a day, that she had when she reached adulthood. If you want to add variety, choose a healthy option, such as rice, pasta, cooked chicken, tuna, white fish, and occasionally cheese or sausages. As always, the complete kibble is the all-important supplier of the dog's needs.

Keep a close check on your Boxer so that you can spot any problems at an early stage.

TOP TIPS FOR HEALTHY BOXERS

- Ensure you start with healthy breeding lines – including heart-tested parents.
- Maintain a regular worming and vaccination regime.
- Provide early training to ensure the dog fits well into family life and the community.
- Give regular health checks – including eyes, ears, nose, mouth/teeth, skin and feet.
- Provide a stimulating mix of daily exercise and education.
- Provide a balanced diet with some variety – but no excessive treats!

In terms of exercise, again, this does not really need to change much depending on your Boxer's health and mobility. An older dog will enjoy the stimulation of being taken out to different places – just make sure you monitor his progress and be aware when he starts to slow up and needs a reduced amount of exercise.

HEALTH CHECKS

The older dog's general health needs to be monitored regularly. You need to take note of changing habits, monitoring how your Boxer approaches and eats his food, and how often he urinates and defecates, which are indicators of good health. If you spot signs of trouble at an early stage, there is a better chance of successful treatment. Just as you have cared for your Boxer throughout his adult life, continue to keep a check on ears, eyes, nose, teeth, feet and nails, and keep up to date with worming and flea prevention.

ILLNESS IN OLD AGE

There will be dogs that seem to get old before their time; they may develop stiff or sore joints, they may become incontinent (more common in spayed bitches), they may develop lumps/tumours that need to be removed, or they may develop a heart condition. In most cases, these conditions can be treated, improved and managed into later life. For more information, see Chapter Eight: Happy and Healthy.

The Boxer is prone to heart and cancer problems, both of these are being tackled by the Boxer Breed Council and the Animal Health Trust, with schemes in place supported by breeders and the Kennel Club to attempt to eliminate genetic problems from the breed. However, this is a long and difficult task and will take many years.

So in the short-term, as advised above, check the history of the puppy you buy, or any history available for a Boxer that has been rehomed, and always buy from reputable breeders that have their stock heart-tested.

It is essential that the elderly Boxer enjoys a good quality of life.

SAYING GOODBYE

For your treasured Boxer there will never really be a right time to end his life, but we must address the situations that would call for such action. If your dog has been in an accident, you will be heavily reliant on your vet for advice and long-term prognosis. You may also have to consider costs, especially if the dog is not insured. If your dog has been diagnosed with an incurable disease (cancer, for example), it may be possible to control the condition for a while, but the time will come when you will need to put the dog's health and quality of life before your need to keep him alive.

Consider the following:

- Is the dog in pain? If so, for how long? Is it curable?
- Is the dog uncomfortable?
- Is the dog unhappy?
- Is the dog eating?
- Is the dog incontinent, or aware when he needs to go to the toilet?

- Am I happy to see the dog in this condition?

A Boxer likes to be clean, dignified, warm, comfortable and loved; he also likes to be active and to enjoy his food and your company. When the quality of life becomes very poor, it really is kinder to let him go. A Boxer who is unable to walk, for example, cannot enjoy life. You need to be very sure that you are not keeping the dog alive for your own reasons. Try to see life from your Boxer's perspective: you know his personality and what makes him happy.

The time may come when you have to take a deep breath, look at the facts, assess your Boxer's quality of life, and extend your love by giving him a release from pain and misery. Euthanasia is not painful; an injection into the vein is all it takes and the dog will pass quietly away, going to sleep in your arms. You can discuss euthanasia with your vet, who can explain exactly what he will do.

The dog can be individually cremated so that you have his ashes to keep or to scatter, or he can be given a general cremation with other deceased pets. You can opt to bury your dog in your garden; the vet will give you advice on this if it is your chosen preference. It is tough thinking about such matters, but taking on a Boxer means caring for him when he is young and when he is old, in sickness and in health – and always putting his needs first.

When you say goodbye to your Boxer, it leaves a terrible gap, but try to remember the good times – and there will be many, I know.

Boxers are like our best friends: they can never be replaced, but a new playmate in the house can aid recovery for all the family.

TRAINING AND SOCIALISATION

Chapter 6

When you decided to bring a Boxer into your life, you probably had dreams of how it was going to be: long walks together, cosy evenings with a Boxer lying devotedly at your feet, and, whenever you returned home, there would always be a special welcome waiting for you.

There is no doubt that you can achieve all this – and much more – with a Boxer, but like anything that is worth having, you must be prepared to put in the work. A Boxer, regardless of whether it is a puppy or an adult, does not come ready trained, understanding exactly what you want and fitting perfectly into your lifestyle. A Boxer has to learn his place in your family and he must discover what is acceptable behaviour.

We have a great starting point

in that the Boxer has an outstanding temperament. The breed thrives on human companionship and your Boxer will enjoy the quality time he spends with you in training sessions. He is also highly intelligent – he has a large skull with plenty of brain room – so we have all the ingredients needed to produce a well-trained, well-behaved companion.

THE FAMILY PACK

Dogs have been domesticated for some 14,000 years, but, luckily for us, they have inherited and retained behaviour from their distant ancestor – the wolf. A Boxer may never have lived in the wild, but he is born with the survival skills and the mentality of a meat-eating predator who hunts in a pack. A wolf living in a pack owes its existence to mutual co-operation and an acceptance of a hierarchy, as this ensures

both food and protection. A domesticated dog living in a family pack has exactly the same outlook. He wants food, companionship, and leadership – and it is your job to provide for these needs.

YOUR ROLE

Theories about dog behaviour and methods of training go in and out of fashion, but in reality, nothing has changed from the day when wolves ventured in from the wild to join the family circle. The wolf (and equally the dog) accepts a subservient place in the family pack in return for food and protection. In a dog's eyes, you are his leader, and he relies on you to make all the important decisions. This does not mean that you have to act like a dictator or a bully. You are accepted as a leader, without argument, as long as you have the right credentials.

Do you have what it takes to be a firm, fair and consistent leader?

HOW TO BE A GOOD LEADER

There are a number of guidelines to follow to establish yourself in the role of leader in a way that your Boxer understands and respects. If you have a puppy, you may think you don't have to take this on board for a few months, but that would be a big mistake. Start as you mean to go on, and your pup will be quick to find his place in his new family.

- **Keep it simple:** Decide on the rules you want your Boxer to obey and always make it 100 per cent clear what is acceptable, and what is unacceptable, behaviour.

- **Be consistent:** If you are not consistent about enforcing rules, how can you expect your Boxer to take you seriously? There is nothing worse than allowing your Boxer to jump up at you one moment and then scolding him the next time he does it because you are wearing your best clothes. As far as the Boxer is concerned, he may as well try it on, as he can't predict your reaction.

- **Get your timing right:** Whether you are rewarding your Boxer or reprimanding him, you must respond within one to two seconds otherwise the dog will not link his behaviour with your reaction (see page 88).

- **Read your dog's body language:** Find out how to read body language and facial expressions (see page 86) so that you understand your Boxer's feelings and intentions.

The first part of the job is easy. You are the provider, and you are therefore respected because you supply food. In a Boxer's eyes, you must be the ultimate hunter because a day never goes by when you cannot find food. The second part of the leader's job description is straightforward, but for some reason we find it hard to achieve. In order for a dog to accept his place in the family pack he must respect his leader as the decision-maker. A low-ranking pack animal does not question authority; he is perfectly happy to see someone else shoulder the responsibility. Problems will only arise if you cut a poor figure as leader and the dog feels he should mount a challenge for the top-ranking role.

A dog pays more attention to body language than to verbal communication. This Boxer is deaf and responds purely to signs.

- **Be aware of your own body language:** You can help your dog to learn by using your body language to communicate with him. For example, if you want your dog to come to you, open your arms out and look inviting. If you want your dog to stay, use a hand signal (palm flat, facing the dog) so you are effectively 'blocking' his advance.

- **Tone of voice:** Dogs are very receptive to tone of voice, so you can use your voice to praise him or to correct undesirable behaviour. If you are pleased with your Boxer, praise him to the skies in a warm, happy voice. If you want to stop him raiding the bin, use a deep, stern voice

when you say "No".

- **Give one command only:** If you keep repeating a command, or keeping changing it, your Boxer will think you are babbling and will probably ignore you. If your Boxer does not respond the first time you ask, make it simple by using a treat to lure him into position, and then you can reward him for a correct response.

- **Daily reminders:** A young, exuberant Boxer is apt to forget his manners from time to time, and an adolescent dog may attempt to challenge your authority (see page101). Rather than coming down on your Boxer like a ton of bricks when he does something

wrong, try to prevent bad manners by daily reminders of good manners. For example:

  i Do not let your dog barge ahead of you when you are going through a door.

  ii Do not let him leap out of the car the moment you open the door (which could be potentially lethal, as well as being disrespectful).

  iii Do not let him eat from your hand when you are at the table.

  iv Do not let him 'win' a toy at the end of a play session and then make off with it. You 'own' his toys, and you must end every play session on your terms.

Dogs of other breeds find it hard to 'read' the Boxer's facial expression.

UNDERSTANDING YOUR BOXER

Body language is an important means of communication between dogs, which they use to make friends, to assert status, and to avoid conflict. It is important to get on your dog's wavelength by understanding his body language and reading his facial expressions.

- A positive body posture and a wagging tail indicate a happy, confident dog.
- A crouched body posture, with ears back, show that a dog is being submissive. A dog may do this when he is being told off or if a more assertive dog approaches him. A bold dog will stand tall, looking strong and alert. His ears will be forward and his tail will be held high.
- A dog who raises his hackles (lifting the fur along his topline) is trying to look as scary as possible. This may be the prelude to aggressive behaviour, but, in many cases, the dog is apprehensive and is unsure how to cope with a situation.
- A playful dog will go down on his front legs while standing on his hind legs in a bow position. This friendly invitation says: "I'm no threat, let's play."
- A truly dominant dog will meet other dogs with a hard stare. If he is challenged, he may bare his teeth and growl, and the corners of his mouth will be drawn forward. His ears will be forward and he will appear tense in every muscle (see page 104).
- A nervous dog will often show aggressive behaviour as a means of self-protection. If threatened, this dog will lower his head and flatten his ears. The corners of his mouth may be drawn back, and he may bark or whine.

MEETING DOGS

The body posture of a dominant dog, with an upright stance, can be seen in all breeds, and is clearly understood when two dogs meet. However, this stance

Boxers understand each other – but they need to be socialised with other breeds.

appears to be inherent among Boxers. Typically, when a Boxer meets another dog, he will stand tall and look directly ahead, often with a hard stare. In this situation, the Boxer is not necessarily being dominant, but he is showing alpha male behaviour. As a result, Boxers can get into trouble meeting dogs, even when their intentions are friendly. At the other extreme, the Boxer is a very lively bouncy dog, and once he has assessed another dog, he can be very boisterous, which some

dogs do not appreciate.

It has been said that the Boxer is hard to 'read' because of his facial expression, which is rather owl-like and shows little variation, and also because of the docked tail, which cannot convey signals such as submissiveness. However, most dogs will pick up other signs and would not be reliant on the tail to assess status.

To give your Boxer the best chance of getting on well with other dogs, take him to socialisation classes so that he has

the opportunity to meet lots of different breeds. This will teach him to temper his body language so that he gives off friendly signals, and to inhibit his play so he is not too boisterous.

As a Boxer owner, be aware of situations when you take your dog out in public. If your Boxer is off the lead, be vigilant if a strange dog approaches. It is much better to be in charge and call your dog back to you, rather than standing by and allowing an incident to develop.

A Boxer may weigh up a situation before he is ready to approach with confidence.

MEETING PEOPLE

The Boxer is a friendly, confident dog, but he tends to be wary when first meeting people; he likes to weigh up a situation before reacting. If someone approaches a Boxer without giving him a chance to 'think first', he may react by cringing and trying to hide behind his owner's legs, or he may go to the opposite extreme and throw himself at the person! The best approach is to stand still, give the Boxer a chance to make his evaluation, and within seconds he will be your best friend for life!

GIVING REWARDS

Why should your Boxer do as you ask? If you follow the guidelines given above, your Boxer should respect your authority, but what about the time when he is playing with a new doggy friend or has found a really enticing scent? The answer is that you must always be the most interesting, the most attractive, and the most irresistible person in your Boxer's eyes. It would be nice to think you could achieve this by personality alone, but most of us need a little extra help. You need to find out what is the biggest reward for your dog. Your Boxer may be a real foodie and love working for food treats, or you may find that he is strongly motivated by a toy. Trainers tend to find that it is easier to work with food treats, as the Boxer has a tendency to become very toy obsessed – but the most important issue is that you find a reward that your Boxer really wants.

When you are teaching a dog a new exercise, you should reward him frequently. When he knows the exercise or command, reward him randomly so that he keeps on responding to you in a positive manner. If your dog does something extra special, like leaving his canine chum mid-play in the park, make sure he really knows how pleased you are by giving him a handful of treats or throwing his ball a few extra times. If he gets a bonanza reward, he is more likely to come back on future occasions, because you have proved to be even more rewarding than his previous activity.

TOY MANNERS

If you are going to reward your Boxer with a toy, you will need to establish some ground rules:

- The toy that is used for training only comes out at training sessions.
- You are in control of the toy at all times.
- If you are playing a tug game, you need to teach a command, such as "Leave", so that your Boxer knows when to give up the toy. It may help if you put your Boxer in a Down before you give this command so that he is in a submissive position.
- You initiate play sessions, and you decide when to end the game.

If you follow these rules, you can use the toy as an effective training aid – and your Boxer will thoroughly enjoy his training sessions.

TOP TREATS

Some trainers grade treats depending on what they are asking the dog to do. A dog may get a low-grade treat, such as a piece of dry food, to reward good behaviour on a random basis, such as sitting when you open a door or allowing you to examine his teeth. But high-grade treats, which may be cooked liver, sausage or cheese, are reserved for training new exercises or for use in the park when you want a really good recall. Whatever type of treat you use, remember to subtract it from your Boxer's

Be firm when establishing the rules of the game, and a toy can become a valuable training aid.

daily ration. Fat Boxers are lethargic, prone to health problems, and will almost certainly have a shorter life expectancy. Reward your Boxer, but always keep a check on his figure!

HOW DO DOGS LEARN?

It is not difficult to get inside your Boxer's head and understand how he learns, as it is not dissimilar to the way we learn. Dogs learn by conditioning: they find out that specific behaviours produce specific consequences. This is known as operant conditioning or consequence learning. Consequences have to be immediate or clearly linked to the behaviour, as a dog sees the world in terms of action and result. Dogs will quickly learn if an action has a bad consequence or a good consequence.

Dogs also learn by association. This is known as classical conditioning or association learning. It is the type of learning made famous by Pavlov, a psychologist who experimented with dogs. Pavlov presented dogs with food and measured their salivary response (how much they drooled). Then he rang a bell just before presenting the food. At first, the dogs did not salivate until the food was presented. But after a while they learnt that the sound of the bell meant that food was coming, and so they salivated when they heard the bell. A dog needs to learn the association in order for it to have any meaning. For example, a dog that has never seen a lead before will be completely indifferent to it. A dog that has learnt that a lead means he is going for a walk will get excited the second he sees the lead; he has learnt to associate a lead with a walk.

BE POSITIVE

The most effective method of training dogs is to use their ability to learn by consequence and to teach that the behaviour you want produces a good consequence. For example, if you ask your Boxer to "Sit", and reward him with a treat, he will learn that it is worth his while to sit on command because it will lead to a treat. He is far more likely to repeat the behaviour, and the behaviour will become stronger, because it results in a positive outcome. This method of training is known as positive reinforcement, and it generally leads to a happy, co-operative dog that is willing to work, and a handler who has fun training their dog.

The opposite approach is

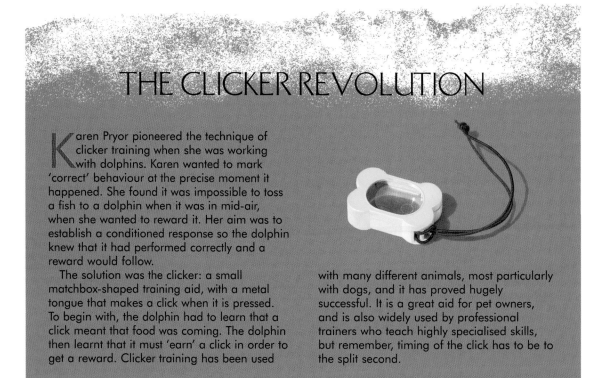

THE CLICKER REVOLUTION

Karen Pryor pioneered the technique of clicker training when she was working with dolphins. Karen wanted to mark 'correct' behaviour at the precise moment it happened. She found it was impossible to toss a fish to a dolphin when it was in mid-air, when she wanted to reward it. Her aim was to establish a conditioned response so the dolphin knew that it had performed correctly and a reward would follow.

The solution was the clicker: a small matchbox-shaped training aid, with a metal tongue that makes a click when it is pressed. To begin with, the dolphin had to learn that a click meant that food was coming. The dolphin then learnt that it must 'earn' a click in order to get a reward. Clicker training has been used with many different animals, most particularly with dogs, and it has proved hugely successful. It is a great aid for pet owners, and is also widely used by professional trainers who teach highly specialised skills, but remember, timing of the click has to be to the split second.

In order to give yourself the best chance of success, find a training area that is free from distractions.

negative reinforcement. This is far less effective and often results in a poor relationship between dog and owner. In this method of training, you ask your Boxer to "Sit", and, if he does not respond, you deliver a sharp yank on the training collar or push his rear to the ground. The dog learns that not responding to your command has a bad consequence, and he may be less likely to ignore you in the future. However, it may well have a bad consequence for you, too. A dog that is treated in this way may associate harsh handling with the handler and become aggressive or fearful. Instead of establishing a pattern of willing co-operation, you are establishing a relationship built on coercion.

GETTING STARTED

As you train your Boxer, you will develop your own techniques as you get to know what motivates him. You may decide to get involved with clicker training or you may prefer to go for a simple command-and-reward formula. It does not matter what form of training you use, as long as it is based on positive, reward-based methods. There are a few important guidelines to bear in mind when you are training your Boxer:

- Find a training area that is free from distractions, particularly when you are just starting out.
- Keep training sessions short, especially with young puppies that have very short attention spans.

- Do not train if you are in a bad mood or if you are on a tight schedule – the training session will be doomed to failure.
- If you are using a toy as a reward, make sure it is only available when you are training. In this way it has an added value for your Boxer.
- If you are using food treats, make sure they are bite-size and easy to swallow; you don't want to hang about while your Boxer chews on his treat.
- All food treats must be deducted from your Boxer's daily food ration.
- If your Boxer is finding an exercise difficult, try not to get frustrated. Go back a step and praise him for his effort. You will probably find he is more successful when you try again

at the next training session.

- Always end training sessions on a happy, positive note. Ask your Boxer to do something you know he can do – it could be a trick he enjoys performing – and then reward him with a few treats or an extra-long play session.
- Remember, training can take place at any place and at any time – it does not have to be reserved to a formal session. If you are in the kitchen waiting for the kettle to boil, or in the sitting room waiting for a TV

programme to start, ask your Boxer to perform a simple exercise, such as a Sit or a Down. It keeps your dog mentally alert, and it also teaches him to work in lots of different places.

- Make training fun – the Boxer has an exuberant love of life, and the more fun he is having, the better he will perform – some Boxers will work for love alone...

In the exercises that follow, clicker training is introduced and

followed, but all the exercises will work without the use of a clicker.

INTRODUCING A CLICKER

This is dead easy, and your ever-hungry Boxer will learn about the clicker in record time! It can be combined with attention training, which is a very useful tool and can be used on many different occasions.

- Prepare some treats and go to an area that is free from distractions. When your Boxer stops sniffing around and looks at you, click and reward by throwing him a treat. This means he will not crowd you, but will go looking for the treat. Repeat a couple of times. If your Boxer is very easily distracted, you may need to start this exercise with the dog on a lead.
- After a few clicks, your Boxer understands that if he hears a click, he will get a treat. He must now learn that he must 'earn' a click. This time, when your Boxer looks at you, wait a little longer before clicking, and then reward him. If your Boxer is on a lead but responding well, try him off the lead.
- When your Boxer is working for a click and giving you his attention, you can introduce a cue or command word, such as "Watch". Repeat a few times, using the cue. You now have a Boxer that understands the clicker and will give you his attention when you ask him to "Watch".

It does not take long for a dog to learn that the sound of the clicker means that a reward is coming.

In time, your Boxer will respond to a verbal command rather than being lured by a treat.

To begin with, lower a treat towards the ground so your Boxer follows it and goes into the Down position.

TRAINING EXERCISES

THE SIT
This is the easiest exercise to teach, so it is rewarding for both you and your Boxer.

- Choose a tasty treat and hold it just above your puppy's nose. As he looks up at the treat, he will naturally go into the Sit. As soon as he is in position, reward him.
- Repeat the exercise, and when your pup understands what you want, introduce the "Sit" command.
- You can practise at mealtimes by holding out the bowl, waiting for your dog to sit, and then putting the bowl down immediately. Most Boxers learn this one very quickly!

THE DOWN
Work hard at this exercise because a reliable Down is useful in many different situations, and an instant Down can be a lifesaver.

- You can start with your dog in a Sit, or it is just as effective to teach it when the dog is standing. Hold a treat just below your puppy's nose, and slowly lower it towards the ground. The treat acts as a lure, and your puppy will follow it, first going down on his forequarters, and then bringing his hindquarters down as he tries to get the treat.
- Make sure you close your fist around the treat, and only reward your puppy with the treat when he is in the correct position. If your puppy is reluctant to go Down, you can apply gentle pressure on his shoulders to encourage him to go into the correct position.
- When your puppy is following the treat and going in to position, introduce a verbal command.
- Build up this exercise over a period of time, each time waiting a little longer before giving the reward, so the puppy learns to stay in the Down position.

Work on getting a really positive response to recall.

BRACE YOURSELF

A word of warning from an experienced Boxer owner:
When you call your Boxer to you, remember to stand perfectly still as he hurtles towards you at the speed of an express train, with no particular intention of stopping. He will take great delight in skimming your legs by a hair's breadth as he hurtles past, before skidding to a halt ten yards behind you and returning with a big grin on his face! One slight move in either direction could leave you prostrate on the floor, with the breath knocked out of you, and your best friend jumping all over you because he thinks that this is some sort of new game that you are playing!

THE RECALL

The enthusiastic Boxer rarely has a problem with Recalls – it is more a matter of curbing his enthusiasm.

• You can start teaching the Recall from the moment your puppy arrives home. He will naturally follow you, so keep calling his name, and reward him when he comes to you.

• Practise in the garden, and, when your puppy is busy exploring, get his attention by calling his name. As he runs towards you, introduce the verbal command "Come". Make sure you sound happy and exciting, so your puppy wants to come to you. When he responds, give him lots of praise.

• If your puppy is slow to respond, try running away a few paces or jumping up and down. It doesn't matter how silly you look, the key issue is to get your puppy's attention, and then make yourself irresistible!

• In a dog's mind, coming when called should be regarded as the best fun because he knows he is always going to be rewarded. Never make the

SECRET WEAPON

You can build up a strong recall by using another form of association learning. Buy a whistle, and when you are giving your Boxer his food, peep on the whistle. You can choose the type of signal you want to give: two short peeps or one long whistle, for example. Within a matter of days, your dog will learn that the sound of the whistle means that food is coming.

Now transfer the lesson outside. Arm yourself with some tasty treats and the whistle. Allow your Boxer to run free in the garden, and, after a couple of minutes, use the whistle. The dog has already learnt to associate the whistle with food, so he will come towards you. Immediately reward him with a treat and lots of praise. Repeat the lesson a few times in the garden so you are confident that your dog is responding

before trying it in the park. Make sure you always have some treats in your pocket when you go for a walk, and your dog will quickly learn how rewarding it is to come to you. But be sensible: if there is something really exciting going on – like a football match in the park – delay letting your Boxer off lead so you are 100 per cent confident he will come back to you.

mistake of telling your dog off, no matter how slow he is to respond, as you will undo all your previous hard work.

- When you are free-running your dog, make sure you have his favourite toy or a pocket full of treats so you can reward him at intervals throughout the walk when you call him to you. Do not allow your dog to free-run and only call him back at the end of the walk to clip his lead on. An intelligent Boxer will soon realise that the Recall means the end of his walk, and then the end of fun – so who can blame him for

not wanting to come back?

TRAINING LINE
This is the equivalent of a very long lead, which you can buy at a pet store, or you can make your own with a length of rope. The training line is attached to your Boxer's collar and should be around 15 feet (4.5 metres) in length.

The purpose of the training line is to prevent your Boxer from disobeying you so that he never has the chance to get into bad habits. For example, when you call your Boxer and he ignores you, you can immediately pick

up the end of the training line and call him again. By picking up the line you will have attracted his attention, and if you call in an excited, happy voice, your Boxer will come to you. The moment he comes to you, give him a tasty treat so he is instantly rewarded for making the 'right' decision.

The training line is very useful when your Boxer becomes an adolescent and is testing your leadership. When you have reinforced the correct behaviour a number of times, your dog will build up a strong recall and you will not need to use a training line.

WALKING ON A LOOSE LEAD

This is a simple exercise, which baffles many Boxer owners. In most cases, owners are too impatient, wanting to get on with the expedition rather than training the dog to walk on a lead. Take time with this one; the Boxer is a strong dog, and a Boxer that pulls on the lead is no pleasure to own.

- In the early stages of lead training, allow your puppy to pick his route and follow him. He will get used to the feeling of being 'attached' to you, and has no reason to put up any resistance.
- Next, find a toy or a tasty treat and show it to your puppy. Let him follow the treat/toy for a few paces, and then reward him.
- Build up the amount of time your pup will walk with you, and when he is walking nicely by your side, introduce the verbal command "Heel" or "Close". Give lots of praise when your pup is in the correct position.
- When your pup is walking alongside you, keep focusing his attention on you by using his name, and then rewarding him when he looks at you. If it is going well, introduce some changes of direction.
- Do not attempt to take your puppy out on the lead until you have mastered the basics at home. You need to be confident that your puppy accepts the lead, and will focus his attention on you, when requested, before you face the challenge of a busy environment.
- As your Boxer gets bigger and stronger, he may try to pull on the lead, particularly if you are heading somewhere he wants to go, such as the park. If this happens, stop, call your dog to you, and do not set off again until he is in the correct position. If necessary, turn in the opposite direction and walk for a few paces with your dog in the Heel position. It may take time, but your Boxer

The Boxer is a strong dog, so it is important that he learns to walk on the lead without pulling.

will eventually realise that it is more productive to walk by your side than to pull ahead.

You may find that, with training, your Boxer responds instantly to the "Heel" or "Close" command, but, four or five strides later, he is out in front. All you can do is to keep stopping or changing direction, so that your dog returns to your side. Boxers are obedient, but not blindly so, and having done as requested, the average Boxer sees no point in repeating it, as there is so much more to be doing!

STAYS

This may not be the most exciting exercise, but it is one of the most useful. There are many occasions when you want your Boxer to stay in position, even if it is only for a few seconds. The classic example is when you want your Boxer to stay in the back of the car until you have clipped on his lead. Some trainers use the verbal command "Stay" when the dog is to stay in position for an extended period of time, and "Wait" if the dog is to stay in position for a few seconds until you give the next command. Others trainers use a universal "Stay" to cover all situations. But there is a danger that your dog will confuse "Stay" with "Stand" or "Sit", so "Wait" is probably a more powerful word to use. It all comes down to personal preference, and as long as you are consistent, your dog will understand the command he is given.

Build up the Stay exercise in easy stages.

- Put your puppy in a Sit or a Down, and use a handsignal (flat palm, facing the dog) to show he is to stay in position. Step a pace away from the dog. Wait a second, step back and reward him. If you have a lively pup, you may find it easier to train this exercise on the lead.
- Repeat the exercise, gradually increasing the distance you can leave your dog. When you return to your dog's side, praise him quietly, and release him with a command, such as "OK".
- Remember to keep your body language very still when you are training this exercise, and avoid eye contact with your dog. Work on this exercise over a period of time, and you will build up a really reliable Stay.

SOCIALISATION

While your Boxer is mastering basic obedience exercises, there is other, equally important, work to do with him. A Boxer is not only becoming a part of your home and family, he is becoming a member of the community. He needs to be able to live in the outside world, coping calmly with every new situation that comes his way. It is your job to introduce him to as many different experiences as possible, and encourage him to behave in an appropriate manner.

In order to socialise your Boxer effectively, it is helpful to understand how his brain is developing, and then you will get a perspective on how he sees the world.

CANINE SOCIALISATION (Birth to 7 weeks)

This is the time when a dog learns how to be a dog. By interacting with his mother and his littermates, a young pup learns about leadership and submission. He learns to read body posture so that he understands the intentions of his mother and his siblings. A puppy that is taken away from his litter too early may always have behavioural problems with other dogs, either being fearful or aggressive.

SOCIALISATION PERIOD (7 to 12 weeks)

This is the time to get cracking and introduce your Boxer puppy to as many different experiences as possible. This includes meeting different people, other dogs and animals, seeing new sights, and hearing a range of sounds, from the vacuum cleaner to the roar of traffic. At this stage, a puppy learns very quickly and what he learns will stay with him for the rest of his life. This is the best time for a puppy to move to a new home, as he is adaptable and ready to form deep bonds.

FEAR-IMPRINT PERIOD (8 to 11 weeks)

This occurs during the socialisation period, and it can be the cause of problems if it is not handled carefully. If a pup is exposed to a frightening or painful experience, it will lead to lasting impressions. Obviously, you will attempt to avoid frightening situations, such as

A young puppy needs to learn about the world he is to live in.

your pup being bullied by a mean-spirited older dog, or a firework going off, but you cannot always protect your puppy from the unexpected. If your pup has a nasty experience, the best plan is to make light of it and distract him by offering him a treat or a game. The pup will take the lead from you and will be reassured that there is nothing to worry about. If you mollycoddle him and sympathise with him, he is far more likely to retain the memory of his fear.

SENIORITY PERIOD (12 to 16 weeks)

During this period, your Boxer puppy starts to cut the apron strings and becomes more independent. He will test out his status to find out who is the pack leader: him or you. Bad habits, such as play biting, which may have been seen as endearing a few weeks earlier, should be firmly discouraged. Remember to use positive, reward-based training, but make sure your puppy knows that you are the leader and must be respected.

SECOND FEAR-IMPRINT PERIOD (6 to 14 months)

This period is not as critical as the first fear-imprint period, but it should still be handled carefully. During this time your Boxer may appear apprehensive, or he may show fear of something familiar. You may feel as if you have taken a backwards step, but if you adopt a calm, positive manner, your Boxer will see that there is nothing to be frightened of. Do

Take your Boxer out and about with you so that he reacts calmly in all situations.

not make your dog confront the thing that frightens him. Simply distract his attention and give him something else to think about, such as obeying a simple command, such as "Sit" or "Down". This will give you the opportunity to praise and reward your dog, and will help to boost his confidence.

YOUNG ADULTHOOD AND MATURITY (1 to 4 years)

The timing of this phase depends on the size of the dog: the bigger the dog, the later it is. This period coincides with a dog's increased size and strength, mental as well as physical. Some dogs, particularly those with a

more assertive nature, will test your leadership again and may become aggressive towards other dogs. Firmness and continued training are essential at this time so that your Boxer accepts his status in the family pack.

IDEAS FOR SOCIALISATION

When you are socialising your Boxer, you want him to experience as many different situations as possible. Try out some of the following ideas, which will ensure your Boxer has an all-round education.

If you are taking on a rescued dog and have little knowledge of his background, it is important to work through a programme of socialisation. A young puppy soaks up new experiences like a sponge, but an older dog can still learn. If a rescued dog shows fear or apprehension, treat him in exactly the same way as you would treat a youngster who is going through the second fear-imprint period (see page 99).

- Accustom your puppy to household noises, such as the vacuum cleaner, the television and the washing machine.
- Ask visitors to come to the door, wearing different types of clothing – for example, wearing a hat or a long raincoat, or carrying a stick or an umbrella.
- If you do not have children at home, make sure your Boxer

has a chance to meet and play with them. Go to a local park and watch children in the play area. You will not be able to take your Boxer inside the play area, but he will see children playing and will get used to their shouts of excitement.

- Attend puppy classes. These are designed for puppies between the ages of 12 to 20 weeks, and give puppies a chance to play and interact together in a controlled, supervised environment. As we have seen, this is particularly important for Boxer puppies. Your vet will have details of a local class.
- Take a walk around some quiet streets, such as a residential

area, so your Boxer can get used to the sound of traffic. As he becomes more confident, progress to busier areas.

- Go to a railway station. You don't have to get on a train if you don't need to, but your Boxer will have the chance to experience trains, people wheeling luggage, loudspeaker announcements, and going up and down stairs and over railway bridges.
- If you live in the town, plan a trip to the country. You can enjoy a day out and provide an opportunity for your Boxer to see livestock, such as sheep, cattle and horses. Remember to observe the Countryside Code.

TRAINING CLUBS

There are lots of training clubs to choose from. Your vet will probably have details of clubs in your area, or you can ask friends who have dogs if they attend a club. Alternatively, use the internet to find out more information. But how do you know if the club is any good?

Before you take your dog, ask if you can go to a class as an observer and find out the following:

- What experience does the instructor(s) have?
- Do they have experience with Boxers?
- Is the class well organised, and are the dogs reasonably quiet? (A noisy class indicates an

unruly atmosphere, which will not be conducive to learning.)
- Are there are a number of classes to suit dogs of different ages and abilities?
- Are positive, reward-based training methods used?
- Does the club train for the Good Citizen Scheme (see page 108)?

If you are not happy with the training club, find another one. An inexperienced instructor who cannot handle a number of dogs in a confined environment can do more harm than good.

Join a training class so that your Boxer learns to focus on you despite the distractions of other dogs.

- One of the best places for socialising a dog is at a country fair. There will be crowds of people, livestock in pens, tractors, bouncy castles, fairground rides and food stalls.
- When your dog is over 20 weeks of age, find a training class for adult dogs. You may find that your local training class has both puppy and adult classes.

THE ADOLESCENT BOXER

It happens to every dog – and every owner. One minute you have an obedient well-behaved youngster, and the next you have a boisterous adolescent who appears to have forgotten everything he learnt. This applies equally to males and females, although the type of adolescent behaviour, and its onset, varies between individuals.

In most cases a Boxer male will hit adolescence at around 10-11 months, and his behaviour may remain erratic until he is between 18 months and two years of age. Most owners of Boxer males find the most trying period is between 15-18 months. During his adolescence, a male Boxer may be even more active and bouncy, and he will misbehave as he tests the boundaries. Female Boxers show adolescent behaviour as they approach their first season, which could be at any time between 6-11 months. At this time, a bitch is subject to her hormones and she may be moody and obstinate. If this happens, do not become confrontational. Play it day by day, and provide opportunities when you can reward your Boxer for good behaviour. With a Boxer, it is always better to be positive than negative.

In reality, adolescence is not the nightmare period you may imagine, if you see it from your Boxer's perspective. Just like a teenager, an adolescent Boxer

101

feels the need to flex his muscles and challenge the status quo. He may become disobedient and break house rules as he tests your authority and your role as leader. Your response must be firm, fair and consistent. If you show that you are a strong leader (see page 84) and are quick to reward good behaviour, your Boxer will accept you as his protector and provider.

WHEN THINGS GO WRONG

Positive, reward-based training has proved to be the most effective method of teaching dogs, but what happens when your Boxer does something wrong and you need to show him that his behaviour is unacceptable? The old-fashioned school of dog training used to rely on the powers of punishment and negative reinforcement. A dog who raided the bin, for example, was smacked. Now we have learnt that it is not only unpleasant and cruel to hit a dog, it is also ineffective. If you hit a dog for stealing, he is more than likely to see you as the bad consequence of stealing, so he may raid the bin again, but probably not when you are around.

If he raided the bin some time before you discovered it, he will be even more confused by your punishment, as he will not relate

As your Boxer reaches maturity, he may seek to challenge your authority.

your response to his 'crime'.

A more commonplace example is when a dog fails to respond to a recall in the park. When the dog eventually comes back, the owner puts the dog on the lead and goes straight home to punish the dog for his poor response. Unfortunately, the dog will have a different interpretation. He does not think: "I won't ignore a recall command because the bad consequence is the end of my play in the park." He thinks: "Coming to my owner resulted in the end of playtime – therefore coming to my owner has a bad consequence, so I won't do that again."

There are a number of strategies to tackle undesirable behaviour – and they have nothing to do with harsh handling.

Ignoring bad behaviour: A lot of undesirable behaviour in young Boxers is to do with over-exuberance. This trait is part of the breed's charm, but it can lead to difficult and sometimes dangerous situations. For example, a young Boxer that repeatedly jumps up at visitors will eventually knock someone over unless he is stopped. In this case, the Boxer is seeking attention, and so the best plan is to ignore him. Do not look at him, do not speak to him, and do not push him down – all these actions are rewarding for your Boxer. But someone who turns their back on him and offers no response is plain boring. The moment your Boxer has four feet on the ground, give him lots of praise and maybe a treat. If you repeat this often enough, the Boxer will learn that jumping up does not have any good consequences, such as getting attention. Instead he is ignored. However, when he has all four feet on the ground, he gets loads of attention. He links the action with the consequence, and chooses the action that is most rewarding. You will find that this strategy works well with all attention-seeking behaviour, such as barking, whining or scrabbling at doors. Being ignored is a worst-case scenario for a Boxer, so remember to use it as an effective training tool.

Stopping bad behaviour: There are occasions when you want to call an instant halt to whatever it is your Boxer is doing. He may have just jumped on the sofa, or you may have caught him red-handed in the rubbish bin. He has already committed the 'crime', so your aim is to stop him and to redirect his attention. You can do this by using a deep, firm tone of voice to say "No", which will startle him, and then call him to you in a bright, happy voice. If necessary, you can attract him with a toy or a treat. The moment your Boxer stops the undesirable behaviour and comes towards you, you can reward his good behaviour. You can back this up by running through a couple of simple exercises, such as a Sit or a Down, and rewarding with treats. In this way, your Boxer focuses his attention on you, and sees you as the greatest source of reward and pleasure.

In a more extreme situation, when you want to interrupt undesirable behaviour, and you know that a simple "No" will not do the trick, you can try something a little more dramatic. If you get a can and fill it with pebbles, it will make a really loud noise when you shake it or throw it. The same effect can be achieved with purpose-made

training discs. The dog will be startled and stop what he is doing. The trick is to make sure the dog doesn't see what you are doing so he will not associate the unpleasant noise with you. This gives you the perfect opportunity to be the nice guy, calling the dog to you and giving him lots of praise.

PROBLEM BEHAVIOUR

If you have trained your Boxer from puppyhood, survived his adolescence and established yourself as a fair and consistent leader, you will end up with a brilliant companion dog. The Boxer is a well-balanced dog who rarely has hang-ups. Most Boxers share an exuberant love of life,

The high-spirited Boxer cannot resist jumping up, but this must be curbed as it shows a lack of respect – and can also be dangerous.

and thrive on spending time with their owners.

However, problems may arise unexpectedly, or you may have taken on a rescued Boxer that has established behavioural problems. If you are worried about your Boxer and feel out of your depth, do not delay in seeking professional help. This is readily available, usually through a referral from your vet, or you can find out additional information on the internet (see Appendices for web addresses). An animal behaviourist will have experience in tackling problem behaviour and will be able to help both you and your dog – but do make sure the behaviourist you employ has experience with Boxers.

GUARDING

The Boxer was bred as a guarding breed, and the instinct to protect home and family remains strong in most Boxers. This is rarely a

problem as long as you remain in control. It is in the Boxer's nature to be wary at the approach of strangers, and, typically, a Boxer will stand in front of you when a stranger approaches to block an advance until he has evaluated the situation. If this happens, give your Boxer a few moments and then use a word such as "OK", so that your Boxer understands that you have taken control and he can relax. In the same way, if a visitor comes to the house, supervise the meeting so that your Boxer realises you are happy to welcome visitors into your home.

Guarding behaviour may become undesirable if a dog becomes too dominant and seeks to elevate his status by challenging your authority (see below). If you think your Boxer is becoming too domineering about guarding his home or members of the family, the best course of

action is to receive or intercept the visitors first. Use a word such as "OK" so that your Boxer is reassured that there is no threat. Then stand between your Boxer and the visitors while you deal with the situation. In this way, your Boxer has done his job, but you have relieved him of the responsibility of being in control.

A Boxer may also attempt to guard his food bowl or a favourite toy. If your Boxer is becoming possessive about his food bowl, put the bowl down empty and drop in a little food at a time. Periodically stop dropping in the food, and tell your Boxer to "Sit" and "Wait". Give it a few seconds, and then reward him by dropping in more food. This shows your Boxer that you are the provider of the food, and he can only eat when you allow him to.

If your Boxer is trying to guard a toy, offer a treat, saying something such as "Thank you" as you swap the reward for the toy. Your Boxer will learn that giving up the toy brings a reward – and you are still in control.

ASSERTIVE BEHAVIOUR

If you have trained and socialised your Boxer correctly, he will know his place in the family pack and will have no desire to challenge your authority. As we have seen, adolescent dogs test the boundaries, and this is the time to enforce all your earlier training so your Boxer accepts that he is not top dog.

However, you may have taken on a rescued dog who has not

Caught red-handed! At times like this you want to call an instant halt to what your Boxer is doing.

been trained and socialised, or you may have let your adolescent Boxer rule the roost by allowing him to take charge. In most cases, this type of overly assertive behaviour tends to be more of a problem in male dogs.

Assertive behaviour is expressed in many ways, which may include the following:

- Showing lack of respect for your personal space. For example, your dog will barge through doors ahead of you or jump up at you.
- Getting up on to the sofa or your favourite armchair, and growling when you tell him to get back on the floor.
- Becoming possessive over a toy, or guarding his food bowl by growling when you get too close (see above).
- Growling when anyone approaches his bed or when anyone gets too close to where he is lying.

- Ignoring basic obedience commands.
- Showing no respect to younger members of the family, pushing amongst them, and completely ignoring them.
- Male dogs may start marking (cocking their leg) in the house.
- Aggression towards people (see page 107).

If you see signs of your Boxer becoming too assertive, you must work at lowering his status so that he realises that you are the leader and he must accept your authority. Although you need to be firm, you also need to use positive training methods so that your Boxer is rewarded for the behaviour you want. In this way, his 'correct' behaviour will be strengthened and repeated.

There are a number of steps you can take to lower your Boxer's status. They include:

- Go back to basics and hold daily training sessions. Make sure you have some really tasty treats, or find a toy your Boxer really values and only bring it out at training sessions. Run through all the training exercises you have taught your Boxer. Make a big fuss of him and reward him when he does well. This will reinforce the message that you are the leader and that it is rewarding to do as you ask.
- Teach your Boxer something new; this can be as simple as learning a trick, such as shaking paws. Having something new to think about will mentally stimulate your Boxer, and he will benefit from interacting with you.
- Be 100 per cent consistent with all house rules – your Boxer must never sit on the sofa, and you must never allow him to jump up at you.

The Boxer is a guarding breed, and this behaviour may translate to guarding toys or food.

- Make sure the family eats before you feed your Boxer. Some trainers advocate eating in front of the dog (maybe just a few bites from a biscuit) before starting a training session, so the dog appreciates your elevated status.
- Do not let your Boxer barge through doors ahead of you or leap from the back of the car before you release him. You may need to put your dog on the lead and teach him to "Wait" at doorways, and then reward him for letting you go through first.

Ask your Boxer to "Wait" at doorways rather than barging ahead of you.

If your Boxer is progressing well with his retraining programme, think about getting involved with a dog sport, such as agility or competitive obedience. This will give your Boxer a positive outlet for his energies. However, if your Boxer is still seeking to be assertive, or you have any other concerns, do not delay in seeking the help of an experienced Boxer owner, or a trainer or behaviourist who has extensive knowledge of Boxers.

SEPARATION ANXIETY
The Boxer will generally accept short periods of separation from his owner without becoming anxious, particularly if he is accustomed to the regime from an early age. A new puppy should be left for short periods on his own, ideally in a crate where he cannot get up to any mischief. It is a good idea to leave him with a boredom-busting toy (see page 54) so he will be happily occupied in your absence. When you return, do not rush to the crate and make a huge fuss. Wait a few minutes, and then calmly go to the crate and release your dog, telling him how good he has been. If this scenario is repeated a number of times, your Boxer will soon learn that being left on his own is no big deal.

Problems with separation anxiety are most likely to arise if you take on a rescued dog who has major insecurities. Separation anxiety is expressed in a number of ways, and all are equally distressing for both dog and owner. An anxious dog who is left alone may bark and whine continuously, urinate and defecate, and may be extremely destructive.

There are a number of steps you can take when attempting to solve this problem.

- Put up a baby-gate between adjoining rooms, and leave your dog in one room while you are in the other room. Your dog will be able to see you and hear you – and you can talk to him – but he is learning to cope without being right next to you. Build up the amount of time you can leave your dog in easy stages.
- Buy some boredom-busting toys and fill them with some tasty treats. Whenever you leave your dog, give him a food-filled toy so that he is busy while you are away.
- If you have not used a crate before, it is not too late to start. Make sure the crate is big and comfortable, and train your Boxer to get used to going in his crate while you are in the same room. Gradually build up the amount of time he spends in the crate, and then start leaving the room for short periods. When you return, do not make a fuss of your dog. Leave him for five or 10 minutes before releasing him so that he gets used to your comings and goings.
- Pretend to go out, putting on your coat and jangling keys, but do not leave the house. An anxious dog often becomes

hyped up by the ritual of leave taking, and so this will help to desensitize him.

- It may help if you accustom your Boxer to being left by using a phrase, such as: "I'm going out – you are to stay here." If this is spoken in a quiet, calm manner, the Boxer understands what is happening, and that he has nothing to fear.
- When you go out, leave a radio or a TV on. Some dogs are comforted by hearing voices and background noise when they are left alone.
- Try to make your absences as short as possible when you are first training your dog to accept

being on his own. When you return, do not fuss your dog, rushing to his crate to release him. Leave him for a few minutes, and, when you go to him, remain calm and relaxed so that he does not become hyped up with a huge greeting.

If you take these steps, your dog should become less anxious, and, over time, you should be able to solve the problem. However, if you are failing to make progress, do not delay in seeking help from someone who has experience with the Boxer mentality.

Use a stairgate between rooms so that your Boxer can still see you, but gets used to being on his own.

AGGRESSION

Aggression is a complex issue, as there are different causes and the behaviour may be triggered by numerous factors. It may be directed towards people, but far more commonly it is directed towards other dogs. Aggression in dogs may be the result of:

- Assertive behaviour (see page 104).
- Defensive behaviour: This may be induced by fear, pain or punishment.
- Territory: A dog may become aggressive if strange dogs or people enter his territory (which is generally seen as the house and garden).
- Intra-sexual issues: This is aggression between sexes – male-to-male or female-to-female.
- Parental instinct: A mother dog may

become aggressive if she is protecting her puppies.

A dog who has been well socialised (see page 98) and has been given sufficient exposure to other dogs at significant stages of his development will rarely be aggressive. Obviously if you have taken on an older, rescued dog, you will have little or no knowledge of his background, and if he shows signs of aggression, the cause will need to be determined. It could be caused by a physical problem, so it is vital to find out what is going on, and then determining a suitable course of action. If you feel out of your depth, do not delay in seeking help with someone who has experience with Boxers.

NEW CHALLENGES

If you enjoy training your Boxer, you may want to try one of the many dog activities that are now on offer.

GOOD CITIZEN SCHEME

This is a scheme run by the Kennel Club in the UK and the American Kennel Club in the USA. The schemes promote responsible ownership and help you to train a well-behaved dog who will fit in with the community. The schemes are excellent for all pet owners, and they are also a good starting point if you plan to compete with your Boxer when he is older. The KC and the AKC schemes vary in format. In the UK there are three levels: bronze, silver and gold, with each test becoming progressively more demanding. In the AKC scheme there is a single test.

Some of the exercises include:
- Walking on a loose lead among people and other dogs.
- Recall amid distractions.
- A controlled greeting where dogs stay under control while owners meet.
- The dog allows all-over grooming and handling by his owner, and also accepts being handled by the examiner.
- Stays, with the owner in sight, and then out of sight.
- Food manners, allowing the owner to eat without the dog begging, and taking a treat on command.
- Sendaway – sending the dog to his bed.

The tests are designed to show the control you have over your dog, and his ability to respond correctly and remain calm in all situations. The Good Citizen Scheme is taught at most training clubs. For more information, log on to the Kennel Club or AKC website (see Appendices). The British Boxer Club encourages owners to participate in a temperament tests. For more details, contact the British Boxer Club (see Appendices).

THERAPY DOGS

The Boxer is ideally suited to working as a therapy dog; he is gentle, kind and lovable. Therapy dogs go with their owners to visit residents in a variety of different institutions, which may include hospitals, care homes, and prisons. It is widely acknowledged that interacting with a dog has great therapeutic benefits, and so the work is very rewarding. Therapy dogs are assessed to ensure they have the correct temperament, and their owners must have a good measure of control. For more information on training your Boxer to be a therapy dog, see Appendices.

SHOWING

In your eyes, your Boxer is the most beautiful dog in the world – but would a judge agree? Showing is a highly competitive sport and the expense of

If you are enjoying training your Boxer, why not take on the challenge of a specialist canine sport?

Showing is highly competitive, but it is also an enjoyable day out for you and your Boxer.

travelling to shows and entries has to be taken into consideration. However, many owners get bitten by the showing bug, and their calendar is governed by the dates of the top showing fixtures.

To be successful in the show ring, a Boxer must conform as closely as possible to the Breed Standard, which is a written blueprint describing the 'perfect' Boxer (see Chapter Seven). To get started you need to buy a puppy that has show potential and then train him to perform in the ring. A Boxer will be expected to stand in show pose, gait for the judge in order to show off his natural movement, and to be examined by the judge. This involves a detailed hands-on examination, so your Boxer must be bombproof when handled by strangers.

Many training clubs hold ringcraft classes, which are run by experienced showgoers. At these classes, you will learn how to handle your Boxer in the ring, and you will also find out about rules, procedures and show ring etiquette.

COMPETITIVE OBEDIENCE

Border Collies, Working Sheepdogs and German Shepherds dominate this sport, but there is no doubt that the Boxer has the intelligence to do well in competitive obedience; the challenge is curbing the exuberance and producing the accuracy that is demanded. The classes start off being relatively easy and become progressively more challenging with the handler giving minimal instructions to the dog.

Exercises include:
• Heelwork
• Recall
• Retrieve
• Sendaway

• Stays
• Scent
• Distance control.

Even though competitive obedience requires accuracy and precision, make sure you make it fun for your Boxer, with lots of praise and rewards so that you motivate him to do his best. Many training clubs run advanced classes for those who want to compete in obedience, or you can hire the services of a professional trainer for one-on-one sessions.

AGILITY

This fun sport has grown enormously in popularity over the past few years. If you fancy having a go, make sure you have good control over your Boxer and keep him slim. Agility is a very physical sport, which demands fitness from both dog and handler. A fat Boxer is never

The Boxer is fast and athletic – it's just a matter of getting the control...

going to make it as an agility competitor. You will need to wait until your Boxer is 18 months before you can compete, as it is potentially hazardous to put a young, growing dog under too much physical strain.

In agility competitions, each dog must complete a set course over a series of obstacles, which include:

- Jumps (upright hurdles and long jump)
- Weaves
- A-frame
- Dog walk
- Seesaw
- Tunnels (collapsible and rigid)
- Tyre

WORKING TRIALS

This is a very challenging sport, but it is well suited to the Boxer temperament. The sport consists of three basic components:

- **Control:** Dog and handler must complete obedience exercises, but the work does not have to be as precise as it is in competitive obedience. The advanced classes include guarding/protection exercises.
- **Agility:** The dog must negotiate a 3 ft (0.91 m) hurdle, a 9 ft (2.75 m) long jump, and a 6 ft (1.82 m) upright scale, which is the most taxing piece of dog equipment.

- **Nosework:** The dog must follow a track that has been laid over a set course. The surface may vary, and the length of time between the track being laid and the dog starting work is increased in the advanced classes.

The ladder of stakes are: Companion Dog, Utility Dog, Working Dog, Tracking Dog and Patrol Dog. In the US, tracking is a sport in its own right, and is very popular among Boxer owners.

If you want to get involved in working trials, you will need to find a specialist club or a trainer that specialises in this sport. For

more information, see
Appendices.

FLYBALL

Flyball is a team sport; the dogs
love it, and it is undoubtedly the
noisiest of all the canine sports!

Four dogs are selected to run in
a relay race against an opposing
team. The dogs are sent out by
their handlers to jump four
hurdles, catch the ball from the
flyball box, and then return over
the hurdles. At the top level, this
sport is fast and furious, and
although it is dominated by
Border Collies, reliable Boxers can
make a big contribution. This is
particularly true in multibreed
competitions where the team is
made up of four dogs of different
breeds, and only one can be a
Border Collie or a Working
Sheepdog. Points are awarded to
dogs and teams. Annual awards
are given to top dogs and top
teams, and milestone awards are
given out to dogs as they attain
points throughout their flyballing
careers.

DANCING WITH DOGS

This sport is relatively new, but it
is becoming increasingly popular.
It is very entertaining to watch,
but it is certainly not as simple as
it looks. To perform a
choreographed routine to music
with your Boxer demands a huge
amount of training.

Dancing with dogs is divided
into two categories: heelwork to
music and canine freestyle. In
heelwork to music, the dog must
work closely with his handler and
show a variety of close 'heelwork'

The quality time you spend training your Boxer will enhance your relationship with him.

positions. In canine freestyle, the
routine can be more flamboyant,
with the dog working at a
distance from the handler and
performing spectacular tricks.
Routines are judged on style and
presentation, content and
accuracy.

SUMMING UP

The Boxer is a wonderful
companion dog and thoroughly

deserves his worldwide fan club.
He has an outstanding
temperament; he is a loyal and
loving family dog, and is fun and
rewarding to live with. Make sure
you keep your half of the bargain:
spend time socialising and
training your Boxer, and involving
him in your life, so that you can
be proud to take him anywhere
and he will always be a credit to
you.

THE PERFECT BOXER

When dog showing first began, the early enthusiasts had the onerous task of formulating a Breed Standard, which gave guidelines to the physical qualities and characteristics required to produce the perfect Boxer. In Germany, the Deutscher Boxer Club, formed in Munich in January 1896, held its first show. However, it took a further six years to formulate a Standard and have it agreed – but, after all, this is a man-made breed, a designer dog you may say.

The British Boxer Club was formed in 1936 and the first British Champion was not produced until 1939. Both the British and American Breed Standards for the Boxer are derived from the original German version, but while including a lot of the correct detail for every feature, some clarity may have been lost in translation.

WHAT IS A BREED STANDARD?

A Breed Standard is a set of guidelines used to ensure that the animals produced by a breeder conform to the specifics of the breed. It is also used in competition to judge a given animal against the hypothetical perfect specimen of that breed. My comment here, however, is that a perfect Boxer does not exist, as there will always be at least one element of the dog that just does not quite match the perfect description. There are many that do come extremely close, and these generally go on to become Champions.

The form in which Breed Standards are written differs among the kennel clubs. There is inconsistency in the amount of detail required to describe a particular characteristic, and sometimes even in the wording used for the characteristics. The result is that Breed Standards will differ from country to country, and are open to interpretation. In the show ring, it will come down to a judge's own interpretation of the Standard and the person's individual taste.

The development of the Standard over the years has also taken account of the origins of the Boxer, i.e. bull-baiting, and the changes from that role to today's companion and show dog. While we can read and learn what is included in the Standard of our own country, putting it into practice when judging is not so easy. The way to learn is to compare examples of the breed to the Standard to see where they conform and

The judge must decide which Boxer in the ring comes closest to matching the written description of the ideal Boxer described in the Breed Standard.

where they fall short of what is required. The only place to do this is at dog shows, where you can watch several judges going over the same dogs and generally coming up with similar results. By comparing the top winners of the day to the Standard, you will learn how to interpret the written requirements to the physical examples of the breed.

It takes many years to acquire the experience necessary to judge the breed, which is why today's judges have very exacting stages to go through to judge at Championship show level. This includes the physical judging of dogs, breeding or showing at least three dogs through to gaining their stud book number in the UK, and attending various seminars that cover the theory as well as the practical hands-on knowledge a judge must have. Not an easy task and one that will take many, many years.

ANALYSING THE BREED STANDARD

The aim of this chapter is to analyse the Boxer Breed Standard applicable in the UK, and to compare it to the American Kennel Club Standard, taking note of the FCI Standard where appropriate, so that we may look at the differences between them. Let's first explain what each organisation is responsible for:

The Kennel Club (KC) in the UK was founded in 1873 and is able to offer dog owners an unparalleled source of information, experience and advice on dog welfare, dog health, dog training and dog breeding. The primary objective of the Kennel Club is 'to promote, in every way, the general improvement of dogs'.

The American Kennel Club (AKC) was founded on 17 September 1884 and brought together 12 dedicated sportsmen

who were called to a meeting. Each member of the group was a representative or 'delegate' from a dog club that had, in the recent past, held a benched dog show or had run field trials. This new 'Club of Clubs' was, in fact, the American Kennel Club and became responsible for the AKC stud book and the rules governing dog shows.

The Fédération Cynologique Internationale (FCI) was created on 22 May 1911 with the aim to promote and protect cynology and purebred dogs by any means it considers necessary.

The founding nations of the FCI were:
- Germany (Kartell für das Deutsche Hundewesen en und Die Delegierten Kommission)
- Austria (Osterreichischer Kynologenverband)
- Belgium (Société Royale Saint-Hubert)
- France (Société Centrale Canine de France)
- Netherlands (Raad van Beheer op Kynologisch Gebied in Nederland).

The FCI disappeared due to the First World War, and, in 1921, the Société Centrale Canine de France and the Société Royale Saint-Hubert recreated it. The new articles of association were adopted on 10 April 1921, and on 5 March 1968, the FCI got its legal name by decree.

The FCI is now the World Canine Organisation. It includes 84 members and contract partners (one member per country), which each issues its own pedigrees and trains its own judges. The FCI makes sure that the pedigrees and judges are mutually recognised by all the FCI members.

The KC, AKC, and FCI Standards for Boxers have all been revised several times over the years. The most recent versions are March 2001 for the FCI, July 2007 (with amended first paragraph in 2009) for the Kennel Club, and 2005 for the AKC versions. The information in this chapter is based on those latest versions.

In 2009, following concern about the health of some dog breeds, the Kennel Club in the UK updated all Breed Standards to include the following introductory paragraph:

"A Breed Standard is the guideline which describes the ideal characteristics, temperament and appearance of a breed and ensures that the breed is fit for function. Absolute soundness is essential. Breeders and judges should at all times be careful to avoid obvious conditions or exaggerations which would be detrimental in any way to the health, welfare or soundness of this breed. From time to time certain conditions or exaggerations may be considered to have the potential to affect dogs in some breeds adversely, and judges and breeders are requested to refer to the Kennel Club website for details of any such current issues. If a feature or quality is desirable it should only be present in the right measure."

In the case of the Boxer – the

There are minor differences in the Breed Standards depending on the national ruling body.

only change made to a specific detail in the existing Breed Standard was to introduce the word 'previously' before 'customarily docked' in the section covering the tail.

GENERAL APPEARANCE

KC
The Boxer should have great nobility, smooth coated, medium-sized, square build, strong bone and evident, well developed muscles.

AKC
The ideal Boxer is a medium-sized, square built dog of good substance with short back,

strong limbs and short, tight-fitting coat. His well developed muscles are clean, hard and appear smooth under taut skin. His movements denote energy. The gait is firm, yet elastic, the stride free and ground covering, the carriage proud. Developed to serve as guard, working and companion dog, he combines strength and agility with elegance and style. His expression is alert and temperament steadfast and tractable. The chiseled head imparts to the Boxer a unique individual stamp. It must be in correct proportion to the body. The broad blunt muzzle is the distinctive feature and great value is placed upon its being of proper form and balance with the skull. In judging the Boxer, first consideration is given to general appearance to which attractive color and arresting style contribute. Next is overall balance with special attention devoted to the head, after which the individual body components are examined for their correct construction and efficiency of gait is evaluated.

The major difference here is that the British Standard is concise and to the point, compared to the rather long-winded American version. The AKC Standard does, however, give a much clearer pictorial description, making it easier for the reader to visualise the animal in full. From this basic description of the general appearance, it is quite easy to look at an example of the breed and form an opinion as to

whether it matches this description, whereas the British version does leave a lot to the imagination, particularly with regard to head features and colour. The tight-fitting coat mentioned in the AKC Standard derives from the need for a fighting dog to give his opponent no opportunity to hang on to him.

In the show ring, the general appearance is the first thing a judge looks for – what takes his or her eye as the dogs come into the ring. Many a judge will comment that having caught sight of a striking animal coming in to the ring, they were not disappointed when they went over the dog at close quarters. This is typical of a good-quality Boxer. General appearance should give a good indication of whether the dog has sound construction, is well balanced and is a pleasure to see. We have to be happy that the overall picture is a good one before worrying too much about the individual aspects of the dog. There are many who will say that judges these days fault judge, picking the whole animal apart without looking at the finer qualities the dog may possess.

CHARACTERISTICS AND TEMPERAMENT

KC
Lively, strong, loyal to owner and family, but distrustful of strangers. Obedient, friendly at play, but with guarding instinct. The temperament should be

The Boxer is a square built dog, with a short back and strong limbs.

equable, biddable, fearless, self-assured.

AKC

These are of paramount importance in the Boxer. Instinctively a "hearing" guard dog, his bearing is alert; dignified and self-assured. In the show ring, his behavior should exhibit constrained animation. With family and friends, his temperament is fundamentally playful, yet patient and stoical with children. Deliberate and wary with strangers, he will exhibit curiosity, but most importantly, fearless courage if threatened. However, he responds promptly to friendly overtures honestly rendered. His intelligence, loyal affection and tractability to discipline make him a highly desirable companion. Faults are lack of dignity and alertness, shyness.

There is little difference between the two Standards on these points, although the AKC Standard does take account of behaviour in the show ring. This is important if you plan to show your Boxer, as fear, shyness or too much aggression would be penalised. The character and temperament of the Boxer are what make him such a popular family pet, as he gets on so well in the family environment. The AKC rightly identifies his stoical attitude with children, where he will take relentless pulling around with little fear of aggression from him towards the children.

The Boxer is friendly and self-assured, but his guarding instinct makes him distrustful of strangers.

However, he will guard his family and their property without fear for his own safety.

The show Boxer has to get used to travelling long distances in the car, to sit on a bench at the side of the show ring sometimes for hours at a time, and then to allow a judge to go over him from head to tail, to look in his mouth and to look him straight in the eye. Those who shy away from the judge or show signs of aggression will be penalised, as this shows the Boxer does not have the correct temperament required, which is calm, composed and not jumpy or nervous.

HEAD AND SKULL: Mouth, eyes, ears and expression

KC

Head imparts its unique individual stamp and is in proportion to body, appearing neither light nor too heavy. Skull lean without exaggerated cheek muscles. Muzzle broad, deep and powerful, never narrow, pointed, short or shallow. Balance of skull and muzzle essential, with muzzle never appearing small, viewed from any angle. Skull cleanly covered, showing no wrinkle, except when alerted. Creases present from root of nose running down sides of muzzle. Dark mask confined to muzzle, distinctly contrasting with colour of head, even when white is present.

Lower jaw undershot, curving slightly upward. Upper jaw broad where attached to skull, tapering very slightly to front. Muzzle shape completed by upper lips, thick and well padded, supported by well separated canine teeth of lower jaw. Lower edge of upper lip rests on edge of lower lip, so that chin is clearly perceptible when viewed from front or side. Lower jaw never to obscure front of upper lip, neither should teeth nor tongue be visible when mouth closed.

Top of skull slightly arched, not rounded, nor too flat and broad. Occiput not too pronounced. Distinct stop, bridge of nose never forced back into forehead, nor should it be downfaced. Length of muzzle measured from tip of nose to inside corner of eye is one-third length of head measured from tip of nose to occiput. Nose broad, black, slightly turned up, wide nostrils with well defined line between. Tip of nose set slightly higher than root of muzzle. Cheeks powerfully developed, never bulging.

MOUTH
Undershot jaw, canines set wide apart with incisors (six) in straight line in lower jaw. In upper jaw set in line curving slightly forward. Bite powerful and sound, with teeth set in normal arrangement.

EYES
The eyes should be dark brown, forward looking, not too small, protruding or deeply set. Showing lively, intelligent expression. Dark rims with good pigmentation showing no haw.

EARS
The ears are of moderate size, thin, set wide apart on highest part of skull lying flat and close to cheek in repose, but falling forward with definite crease when alert.

AKC
The beauty of the head depends upon the harmonious proportion of muzzle to skull. The blunt muzzle is 1/3 the length of the head from the occiput to the tip of the nose, and 2/3rds the width of the

The correct proportions of the Boxer head.

skull. The head should be clean, not showing deep wrinkles (wet). Wrinkles typically appear upon the forehead when ears are erect, and are always present from the lower edge of the stop running downward on both sides of the muzzle. The muzzle, proportionately developed in length, width, and depth, has a shape influenced first through the formation of both jawbones, second through the placement of the teeth, and third through the texture of the lips.

The top of the muzzle should not slant down (downfaced), nor should it be concave (dishfaced); however, the tip of the nose should lie slightly higher than the root of the muzzle. The nose should be broad and black and the expression intelligent and alert. The top of the skull is slightly arched, not rounded, flat, nor noticeably broad, with the occiput not overly pronounced. The forehead shows a slight indentation between the eyes and forms a distinct stop with the topline of the muzzle. The cheeks should be relatively flat and not bulge (cheekiness), maintaining the clean lines of the skull as they taper into the muzzle in a slight, graceful curve.

MOUTH
The Boxer bite is undershot, the lower jaw protruding beyond the upper and curving slightly upward. The incisor teeth of the lower jaw are in a straight line, with the canines preferably up front in the same line to give the jaw the greatest possible width. The upper line of the incisors is slightly convex with the corner upper incisors fitting snugly back of the lower canine teeth on each side. Neither the teeth nor the tongue should ever show when the mouth is closed.

The upper jaw is broad where attached to the skull and maintains this breadth, except for a very slight tapering to the front. The lips, which complete the formation of the muzzle, should meet evenly in front. The upper lip is thick and padded, filling out the frontal space created by the projection of the lower jaw, and laterally is supported by the canines of the lower jaw. Therefore, these canines must stand far apart and be of good length so that the front surface of the muzzle is broad and squarish and, when viewed from the side, shows moderate layback. The chin should be perceptible from the side as well as from the front. Any suggestion of an overlip obscuring the chin should be penalized.

EYES
The eyes should be dark brown in color, frontally placed, generous, not too small, too protruding, or too deepset.

The male (right) has a slightly stronger head than the female.

Their mood-mirroring character, combined with the wrinkling of the forehead, gives the Boxer head its unique quality of expressiveness. Third eyelids preferably have pigmented rims.

EARS

Set at the highest points of the sides of the skull, the ears are customarily cropped, cut rather long and tapering, and raised when alert. If uncropped, the ears should be of moderate size, thin, lying flat and close to the cheeks in repose, but falling forward with a definite crease when alert.

The head is the hallmark of the breed and the Standards agree on the correct proportions to the body. Both descriptions here are very full and leave no doubt as to what the owner should be looking for in terms of a good Boxer head. The Boxer head in profile is one of the most striking you will see if the head is correctly proportioned. I like the descriptive words used in the AKC Standard when talking about "beauty" and "harmony", which the Boxer head has in abundance, if it is correctly made.

The AKC Standard requirement for the muzzle to be two-thirds the width of the skull seems more precise than the UK Standard, which merely asks for the muzzle and skull to be balanced. The head has to be in proportion or it loses type and nobility. If the skull is too broad, this may give a Mastiff look to the head. The muzzle should be the same width at the tip, as it is at the inset to the skull, as too narrow or long a muzzle may give it a Great Dane appearance. This look will also be enhanced if there is a lack of stop and rise of skull.

The definite stop between the forehead and the top of the muzzle is another distinct characteristic of the Boxer head. There should not be too deep a cleft between the eyes, as this will give a Bulldog expression. If there is not enough stop, the Boxer will tend to look like the Great Dane or even the Staffordshire Bull Terrier. This is not a desirable look for the Boxer.

Having been bred initially for bull-baiting, where it was necessary to have gripping power to hold on to the bull, the undershot jaw of the Boxer is so different to other breeds where a scissor bite is required. The undershot jaw allowed him to hold on to the bull until it tired and could be dealt with by the hunter he was working for. The shape of this jaw will affect the whole head if it is not correct. It should be wide, and the lower

The cropped ears of the American Boxer give a markedly different appearance to the head and expression.

teeth set in a straight line. This undershot jaw will also give the required chin, which should be evident from all sides. Without a good chin, there will be a lack of expression, whereas if the chin is too evident or the jaw too undershot, there is a chance that the lower teeth will be on view and this is a definite fault.

The UK Standard does not discuss canines specifically compared to the FCI and American Standards, which specify an obtuse angle (moderate layback) with the topline of the muzzle. If the muzzle has width without the correct turn up, it will tend to look too long, whereas if the muzzle is too short, the head will appear too wide. The muzzle should also be well constructed and not overly padded.

Having had one of my own Boxers criticised for her mouth, when the overall appearance and construction of the bitch were correct, a friend said that she couldn't understand why judges put a good dog down for a mouth fault – after all, the dog only eats with its mouth! The judge who fault finds and puts an animal down the line for one aspect where he or she falls short of the Standard, is being rather harsh if the rest of the animal fulfils the required criteria. On the other hand, and in defence of the judge, what has to be remembered is that the judge has to compare each animal to the Standard. If there are two good specimens fighting for one place, then it will be the one with the

obvious fault in one area that is penalised, and the exhibitor must accept that this will be the case. The Boxer bite has to be correct or he would not have the firm grip to carry out the role for which he was bred.

EYES
The eyes of the Boxer should be the mirror to his soul and give the wonderful expression that we all love. If the eyes are not correct in shape, perhaps too narrow or sloping upwards, they will give a mean and menacing expression,

whereas the true Boxer expression will melt your heart.

The eyes should be dark; it is well known that in other parts of Europe, judges have a boxed set of eye colours and will look to see how closely your Boxer matches the correct colouring of dark brown eyes. Eyes that are too light or have an unpigmented third eyelid, giving a 'fried egg' appearance, will often be criticised. Occasionally, however, an unpigmented eyelid will go unnoticed if the eye is tight and the fault perhaps not immediately

Dark-coloured eyes give the melting expression that is so typical of the breed.

visible. There have been Champions in the UK with an unpigmented third eyelid. The overall effect of this normally is to mar the lovely, typical expression and will therefore rarely go unnoticed.

The black mask will also affect the expression; this should only extend as far as the eyes, as any extension to this may give a sombre expression.

EARS

When it comes to the ears of a Boxer, the Standards are comparable; however, in the USA, the ears are customarily cropped. The ears should fall close to the cheeks when not cropped, and should not be too large for the size of the head. The main significance of ears that do not comply with the Standard is the effect they will have on the expression.

Typically, a puppy may have ears that will fly away, but they will usually settle as they stop teething. When I first started showing Boxers, it was common to see young pups with their ears 'in curlers' or taped up with sticky tape to give them the correct creases, but I am pleased to say that no longer seems to happen in the UK, thank goodness!

The forelegs are straight and parallel, with strong bone.

NECK

KC
Round, of ample length, strong, muscular, clean cut, no dewlap. Distinctly marked nape and elegant arch down to withers.

AKC
Round, of ample length, muscular and clean without excessive hanging skin (dewlap). The neck should have a distinctly arched and elegant nape blending smoothly into the withers.

Again, the AKC Standard has a more colourful description of the elegantly arched neck that is so wonderful to see. Dogs without this long neck will appear stuffy and not have the elegance that is so desirable. This seems to be more of a problem in dogs than bitches, where there is more likely to be a natural elegance. The neck must be clean, meaning there should be no loose skin hanging underneath to give a dewlap effect. The neck must run smoothly into the shoulders.

FOREQUARTERS

KC
Shoulders long and sloping, close lying, not excessively covered with muscle. Upper arm long, making right angle to shoulderblade. Forelegs seen from front, straight, parallel, with strong bone. Elbows not too close or standing too far from chest wall. Forearms perpendicular, long and firmly

muscled. Pasterns short, clearly defined, but not distended, slightly slanted.

AKC
The shoulders are long and sloping, close-lying, and not excessively covered with muscle (loaded). The upper arm is long, approaching a right angle to the shoulder blade. The elbows should not press too closely to the chest wall nor stand off visibly from it. The forelegs are long, straight, and firmly muscled, and, when viewed from the front, stand parallel to each other. The pastern is strong and distinct, slightly slanting, but standing almost perpendicular to the ground. The dewclaws may be removed.

Both Standards give a clear impression of what we are looking for. There is no mention of the dewclaws in the British Standard, but the FCI Standard lists them as a fault.

For the neck to fit so well into the shoulders, there has to be good shoulder placement. The shoulder blades should be well laid back; upright shoulders should be avoided, as this will also indicate shortness in the upper arm. The dog may then look heavy in shoulder, giving a barrel effect to his front. Upright shoulders are very hard to breed out.

The front legs should be under the dog with good length to the upper arm. Along with correct angulation, this will produce a

good forechest. One, perhaps, important difference is that the US Standard does not mention strong bone here, and specifies long forelegs. Strength and bone are, however, mentioned in the areas of Substance and Pasterns. The legs should be straight but have strong bone. The elbows should not be seen to stick out when the dog is on the move, creating an ungainly appearance.

BODY

KC
In profile square, length from forechest to rear of upper thigh equal to height at withers.

Chest deep, reaching to elbows. Depth of chest half height at withers. Ribs well arched, not barrel-shaped, extending well to rear. Withers clearly defined. Back short, straight, slightly sloping, broad and strongly muscled. Loin short, well tucked up and taut. Lower abdominal line blends into curve to rear.

AKC
The body in profile is square in that a horizontal line from the front of the forechest to the rear projection of the upper thigh should equal the length of a vertical line dropped from

The Boxer should convey an impression of nobility and endurance.

the top of the withers to the ground. Sturdy, with balanced musculature. Males larger boned than females. The chest is of fair width, and the forechest well-defined and visible from the side. The brisket is deep, reaching down to the elbows; the depth of the body at the lowest point of the brisket equals half the height of the dog at the withers. The ribs, extending far to the rear, are well-arched but not barrel-shaped. The loins are short and muscular. The lower stomach line is slightly tucked up, blending into a graceful curve to the rear. The croup is slightly sloped, flat and broad. The pelvis is long, and in females especially broad.

This is a vigorous breed that should have speed and endurance, whilst maintaining elegance and nobility on the move. The Boxer's body construction needs to be right to achieve this. While the two Standards are similar and cover the same ground, again, the AKC Standard is more descriptive. It also comments on the slightly larger frame of the male over the female, and the pelvis being broader in the female. Loins should be short and muscular. The FCI Standard mentions straight and broad too; however, there may be a terminology issue here.

The AKC mentions the

slightly sloping croup, which is an important aspect of the breed. If the croup slopes too much, the tail will be low set, which spoils the appearance of the Boxer. The low tail set prevents him from having an alert appearance and this will become more apparent in the undocked Boxer, as the tail may well be carried low, giving a cowed appearance.

A Boxer with the correct proportions, as described here, will have a good spring of rib, giving adequate room for his strong heart and lungs. He will have the square appearance that is so typical of the Boxer. The topline will be slightly sloping, giving a line from the withers to the top of the docked tail. The

The hindquarters are strong and well muscled.

chest should reach the elbow or the dog will appear leggy and with too much light showing under the tuck up. There should be a beautiful curved underline to the rear, as without this the Boxer will look quite plain and common.

HINDQUARTERS

KC
Very strong with muscles hard and standing out noticeably under skin. Thighs broad and curved. Broad croup slightly sloped, with flat, broad arch. Pelvis long and broad. Upper and lower thigh long. Good hind angulation; when standing, the stifle is directly under the hip protuberance. Seen from side, leg from hock joint to foot not quite vertical. Seen from behind, legs straight, hock joints clean, with powerful rear pads.

AKC
The hindquarters are strongly muscled, with angulation in balance with that of the forequarters. The thighs are broad and curved, the breech musculature hard and strongly developed. Upper and lower thigh are long. The legs are well-angulated at the stifle, neither too steep nor over-angulated, with clearly defined, well "let down" hock joints.

Viewed from behind, the hind legs should be straight, with hock joints leaning neither in nor out. From the side, the leg below the hock (metatarsus) should be almost perpendicular to the ground, with a slight slope to the rear permissible. The metatarsus should be short, clean, and strong. The Boxer has no rear dewclaws.

Again, there is very little to choose between the Standards. While the hindquarters should be well-angulated, they should not be overly so. They need to be strong and well-muscled to provide the propulsion that the Boxer needs to gallop and run free. Poor back ends are usually indicated by a lack of angulation and this spoils the outline of the Boxer.

The UK Standard does not mention the angle of the hocks, whereas the FCI Standard is very specific about the angle of 140 degrees. The hocks should be parallel, as nothing looks worse than cow-hocks. I remember Marion Ward-Davis (Winuwuk) commenting on my first Boxer at my first Open show. She said that he was cow-hocked, but with more exercise and better handling this could be corrected. His problem was indeed a lack of exercise, but also my poor handling skills! Often, however, this trait is a sign of weakness and lack of muscle, and will result in poor movement. Good, strong quarters will provide the Boxer with the propulsion he needs to drive him forward.

Some pet Boxers have not been docked for a number of years, but the ban on docking has caused great waves in the show world.

FEET

KC
Front feet small and cat-like, with well arched toes, and hard pads; hind feet slightly longer.

AKC
Feet should be compact, turning neither in nor out, with well-arched toes.

Here the British Standard is far more descriptive about what we are looking for: cat-like feet. This does require lots of roadwork to keep the nails short so that the feet can remain small and tight. Flat, splayed feet can mean that there are other construction faults elsewhere. The feet should be straight in front, not turned in or out (Queen Anne style).

TAIL

KC
Previously customarily docked.
Docked: Set on high and carried upward.
Undocked: Set on high and carried gaily, not curled over back. Of moderate thickness. In overall balance to the rest of dog. (Docking has been banned in the UK from 6 April 2007 and therefore the undocked Standard will come in for puppies born after that date.)

AKC
The tail is set high, docked, and carried upward. An undocked tail should be severely penalized.

The FCI Standard is the only one that specifies the tail being left natural, whereas the American

Standard severely penalises an undocked tail. As in other European countries, the British Government has brought in the ban on docking tails from 6 April 2007. This has been a severe blow to the Boxer owner, as we will now lose that familiar short tail so loved in the breed.

Although the UK Kennel Club has asked breed councils to give an indication of what they require in the Breed Standard for the carriage of tails, the Boxer Breed Council has found this difficult to articulate, as it has no working knowledge of how tails will be carried in reality. It remains to be seen whether the wording used above by the Kennel Club will accurately reflect the carriage of the Boxer tail in Britain, or whether it will be amended in due course. As mentioned earlier, the tail set can be affected by the croup, which, if it falls away too much, will result in an unattractive low tail set and should be avoided.

GAIT/MOVEMENT

KC
Strong, powerful with noble bearing, reaching well forward, and with driving action of hindquarters. In profile, stride free and ground covering.

AKC
Viewed from the side, proper front and rear angulation is manifested in a smoothly efficient, level-backed, ground covering stride with a powerful drive emanating from a freely operating rear. Although the front legs do not contribute impelling power, adequate reach should be evident to prevent interference, overlap, or sidewinding (crabbing). Viewed from the front, the shoulders should remain trim and the elbows not flare out. The legs are parallel until gaiting narrows the track in proportion to increasing speed, then the legs come in under the body but should never cross. The line from the shoulder down through the leg should remain straight although not necessarily perpendicular to the ground. Viewed from the rear, a Boxer's rump should not roll. The hind feet should dig in and track relatively true with the front. Again, as speed increases, the normally broad rear track will become narrower. The Boxer's gait should always appear smooth and powerful, never stilted or inefficient.

The British Standard tells us what to look for in correct movement, but gives no indication of what might go wrong here. The AKC Standard, however, is far more descriptive in the things that can go wrong.

For a Boxer to move well, his construction must be right in the first place. With correct balance of front and rear angulation, the Boxer should move with drive.

The judge will assess the Boxer's conformation when he is on the move.

The front legs should extend beyond the head as he moves, and he will have great drive and reach without resorting to over-reaching (front and rear legs crossing each other). When the dog moves towards you, the legs should be straight with no pinning (paws turning in) and the feet should be close to the ground. Paddling of the feet or high stepping is not correct movement for a Boxer.

You will hear comments such as "that Boxer could knit socks whilst on the move". This refers to the hind legs crossing as the dog moves forward and it is not a good action to see. The hind legs should be propelling the dog forward with no evidence of side-stepping. He should run true behind. As his speed increases, the hind legs will move closer together, but this should not result in moving too close or cross-stepping. A Boxer on the move should be a delight to watch and he should hold his topline true at all times.

COAT

KC
Short, glossy, smooth and tight to body.

AKC
Short, shiny, lying smooth and tight to the body.

An overall good condition for the Boxer is essential to achieve a shiny, glossy coat and what goes into the Boxer will reflect in his outward appearance. This is covered in more detail in Chapter 5. Both Standards agree on the appearance of the coat and the tight fit to the body, which again goes back to the origins of the breed and the need for no loose skin for the bull to get hold of.

COLOUR

KC
Fawn or brindle. White markings acceptable not exceeding one-third of ground colour.
Fawn: Various shades from dark deer red to light fawn. Brindle: Black stripes on previously described fawn shades, running parallel to ribs all over body. Stripes contrast distinctly to ground colour, neither too close not too thinly dispersed. Ground colour clear, not intermingling with stripes.

AKC
The colors are fawn and brindle. Fawn shades vary from

Fawn colouring can range from dark deer red to light fawn.

Brindle markings can be on a light fawn ground colour (left), or on a much darker background (right), but they must be clearly defined.

light tan to mahogany. The brindle ranges from sparse but clearly defined black stripes on a fawn background to such a heavy concentration of black striping that the essential fawn background color barely, although clearly, shows through (which may create the appearance of reverse brindling). White markings, if present, should be of such distribution as to enhance the dog's appearance, but may not exceed one-third of the entire coat. They are not desirable on the flanks or on the back of the torso proper. On the face, white may replace part of the otherwise essential black mask, and may extend in an upward path between the eyes, but it must not be excessive, so as to detract from true Boxer expression. The absence of white markings, the so-called "plain" fawn or brindle, is perfectly acceptable, and should not be penalized in any consideration of color. Disqualifications - Boxers that are any color other than fawn or brindle. Boxers with a total of white markings exceeding one-third of the entire coat.

Once again, we find a more detailed description of good and bad in the AKC Standard, where the UK KC Standard is fairly precise. The AKC Standard is the only one that does not specify that the dark mask must be confined to the muzzle, although it does place it on the face. The KC Standard does not mention expression at all; the AKC mentions it in the terms of white markings and not the mask.

The AKC description of the best placing for white markings is in harmony with what we in the UK look for in our Boxers. Too much white, particularly between the eyes, can mar the expression of an otherwise correct head. One thing I dislike seeing is white chest markings that run down completely into the forelegs. This can give the appearance of a wide front, which is probably not the case, but it does spoil the overall appearance.

The judge must consider the overall balance and impression of each dog before making a decision.

SIZE

KC

Height: dogs: 57-63 cms (22^1/$_2$ -25 ins); bitches: 53-59 cms (21-23 ins). Weight: dogs: approximately 30-32 kgs (66-70 lbs); bitches: approximately 25-27 kgs (55-60 lbs).

AKC

Adult males 23 to 25 inches; females 21^1/$_2$ to 23^1/$_2$ inches at the withers. Proper balance and quality in the individual should be of primary importance since there is no size disqualification.

The American Standard indicates a marginally higher starting point for males and females than in the UK by half an inch and an upper limit for females of half an inch more. Their tolerance of those that step outside of the stipulated size criteria is to be welcomed, as a slightly larger or smaller dog of excellent proportion can be more attractive and seem to comply with the Standard more than one that meets the exact height criteria. I believe that in other European countries judges have been known to bring out a measuring stick, something I hope I never have to see!

The AKC Standard makes no mention of weight guidelines, but it is important that the Boxer does not carry more weight than the guidance given in the UK Standard.

FAULTS

KC

Any departure from the foregoing points should be considered a fault and the seriousness with which the fault should be regarded should be in exact proportion to its degree and its effect upon the health and welfare of the dog. **Male animals should have two apparently normal testicles fully descended into the scrotum.**

AKC

The foregoing description is that of the ideal Boxer. Any deviation from the above described dog must be penalized to the extent of the deviation.

I have mentioned as we have gone along the points on which the Boxer may be penalised in the show ring. The priority must be to consider the overall appearance and balance of the dog, which should be pleasing, before going on to consider the finer details. The perfect Boxer does not exist; all we can do is attempt to breed as close to type as possible and hope that one day we breed a Champion!

HAPPY AND HEALTHY

Chapter 8

Your Boxer will enjoy a healthy and happy life, providing that he is given regular exercise and the opportunity for mental stimulation through general training and activities. As well as giving your dog energetic walks, it is important to feed a balanced diet to ensure that he stays at the peak of fitness.

To keep your Boxer healthy, veterinary care is advised, with necessary vaccinations and parasite control. Visits to the veterinary surgeon are required periodically for vaccinations, at which time the vet will give the dog a physical examination, to check for any undisclosed disease. In between times, daily grooming provides the opportunity to get to know the dog's coat and body structure, ensuring that signs of illness can be detected early. Improved diet and routine vaccinations are contributing to a much longer life for all domestic animals, but the owner of the dog has a role to play in everyday health care.

It is important that you really get to know your dog, as in doing so it is easier to identify when he is 'off colour' and needs to be seen by a vet. Visits to the vet should be made when some abnormality may be detected. It is also important to recognise the signs of a healthy dog when you go to buy a puppy.

Think about getting some pet insurance. This has provided the opportunity for extensive tests and procedures to be undertaken on dogs; but there should be an assessment of what each policy will offer and what sort of limits are put on expense, age or hereditary disorders requiring veterinary attention before buying insurance.

PREVENTATIVE CARE

VACCINATIONS
It is best to take all available measures to keep your Boxer healthy; one of the greatest advances in canine practice in the last 50 years has been the development of effective vaccines to prevent diseases. Within living memory dogs died from fits after distemper, virus infections, and, in the last 20 years, many puppies have contracted parvo virus, which, in the early years of the disease, often proved to be fatal. The routine use of a multiple component vaccine, to protect against canine distemper, infectious canine hepatitis, parvovirus and leptospirosis, is generally accepted as the norm. However, there are still local differences in the age the puppy receives its first injection or 'shot'. The timing for the primary vaccine course doses is based on

when the immunity provided by the puppy's mother declines to a level that will not interfere with the immune response. Canine vaccines currently in use in the UK recommend that the final dose of the primary course should be given at 10 or 12 weeks of age, with annual boosters from then on.

With any breed of dog exercised outdoors, this annual dose is especially necessary for protection against potentially fatal leptospira, which occurs in water and where rats have been present. The length of protection provided after two injections for the puppy is not significantly greater than 12 months (challenges after this date results in shedding of leptospires), and for some vaccines it is considered less than 12 months. For the other protection against the viruses a minimum of three

years is possible and here annual boosters are less essential. Further booster vaccination is recommended at intervals decided by the vet with a local knowledge to protect any of those individual dogs who may have low or marginal blood level titres.

Kennel cough is a distressing, infectious disease. It is usually acquired from airborne contact with other dogs, especially those stressed when visiting dog shows or boarding kennels. There are several vaccines available, and again, advice should be obtained from the vet as to which type of protection is appropriate for your dog. The rabies vaccine is necessary for all dogs leaving the United Kingdom, but is routine in many countries, as is the vaccine for Lyme disease in the USA, where it should be discussed with the vet.

PARASITE CONTROL

Routine worming every three months is obligatory to reduce the risk of infection of susceptible humans handling the dog. There is still a high risk of picking up worm eggs in places frequented by other dogs and most wormers have no sustained protection the day after dosing. Repeated worming is necessary for puppies, and, to a lesser extent, for adult dogs. Many puppies are infested with roundworms, but some breeders will start worming the pregnant bitch to reduce the risk to the newborn pups. Worming of the puppy from two weeks, repeated at regular intervals, is advised. This is because the interval should be close to the 'pre-patent period' when eggs will hatch. Roundworms, hookworms, tapeworms and whipworms present different

The breeder will have started a worming programme, which you will need to continue.

threats, while heartworms (which can result from the bite of an infected mosquito), are a particular problem in the south-east Atlantic and Gulf Coasts of the USA. This is another parasite to consider if you are planning to take your dog to mainland Europe, as heartworm is endemic in the Mediterranean area of France and is slowly spreading northwards due to climate change.

The traditional division of wormers and ectoparasiticides has disappeared with the use of products that remove both internal and external parasites. Fleas were the greatest problem for many dog owners, since fleas have a tendency to bite humans. A single flea on the dog's coat can cause persistent scratching and restlessness. Many effective anti-flea preparations are now available, in the form of tablets, coat applications, or residual sprays to apply to carpets and upholstery.

Lice, fleas, Cheyletiella (often referred to as rabbit mite), mites that burrow under the skin and mites on the surface may all cause disease, and are not easily recognised by the eye, but ticks become large and visible as they gorge themselves with the dog's blood. A thorough grooming of your dog each day will detect many of these parasites and preventative action can then be taken, in the form of a powder, a shampoo, a spot-on insecticide, or spray. The use of an impregnated collar is less favoured, and it has been

suggested that the best place to put such a collar is inside the vacuum cleaner bag!

DIET AND EXERCISE

Some Boxers are naturally lean, making it a harder task to keep them looking healthy. It is a good idea to weigh all dogs on a regular basis; the dog that appears thin, but still actively fit, has fewer reserves to fall back on and weighing on a weekly basis can detect further weight loss

before any disastrous change can occur. Each dog should have an ideal weight; and within a narrow range the actual correct weight for the dog will act as a guide.

Obesity has become a major concern for dogs, as well as humans. Appetite suppressants for dogs – mitratapide (Yarvitan) – available from the vet – can now be used as part of an overall weight management programme.

It is your job to keep your Boxer lean and fit.

COAT, EARS AND FEET

The Boxer's coat should be shiny and healthy. Too much confinement indoors with warm room temperatures can lead to loss of coat, and less hair density for outdoor protection. Regular brushing and grooming stimulates the skin, and provides an opportunity for close inspection of it. The condition of the skin and hair contributes to the animal's overall health.

The Boxer is low maintenance as far as grooming is concerned, but you will still need to keep a regular check on his health and wellbeing.

Grooming is essential, as it stimulates the hair growth stage known as anagen, by the removal of dead, shedding hairs. This helps to prevent bareness or bald patches. The removal of any discharge prevents coat matting and skin irritation, and the close inspection of the animal during grooming assists in the early recognition of any problems.

During grooming, daily care and attention should be given to any bony prominences, such as skin folds, feet and claws, eyes and ears, mouth and teeth, anus, vulva and prepuce.

Regular checks for traces of fleas or ticks attached to the skin can prevent itching and hair loss. When grooming the dog, always make a point of checking the ears - both inside and out. Equally, lip folds should be checked for saliva soaking or unpleasant breath smells. Boxers have large lips and saliva may accumulate around the mouth, so healthy teeth are essential to avoid breath odour. Bathing your Boxer will cleanse the coat and remove smells as well as controlling ectoparasites; it will also improve the appearance of the dog before a show.

The pads of the feet should feel quite soft to the touch, and not leathery (hyperkeratinised). The pigment of the foot pads is often similar to the nose colour. Between the toes there is an area of skin that is hairy and contains sebaceous glands used for scent marking; sometimes cysts and swellings develop if the glands become blocked. The skin between the toes is very sensitive to chemical burns, and some alkaline clay soils will provoke inflammation with lameness known as 'pedal eczema'. Warts are sometimes found on the feet of young dogs, especially those kept in kennels. This is often due to the washing of the concrete runs, which leads to the excessive wetting of the dog's feet.

The nails should be of an even length, and not split at the ends. If the nails are too long, they will have to be clipped; great care must be taken to avoid hurting the dog by cutting into the quick. Exercise on hard, concrete surfaces and stone pavements is normally sufficient to keep nails at a reasonable length; tarmac roads and tarred pavements often do not provide enough friction to wear down the nails. Dewclaws, if present, are not a disadvantage to the dog, but, if they grow in a circle, they can penetrate the flesh, causing an infected wound if not shortened.

A TO Z OF COMMON AILMENTS

ALLERGIES

Allergies are now a common problem for many dogs with skin or intestinal disorders. The condition results from an inappropriate immune response by the dog to an antigen substance, either in food or inhaled through the nose. A process of eliminating possible antigens in the diet, or in the environment, may help to find a cause and there are commercial diets available that can help. Medication can be used to suppress the allergic response and both antihistamines and steroids may be tried before the most suitable treatment is found.

ANAL DISORDERS – ANAL SACCULITIS, ADENOMATA

Modern diets are often blamed for the high incidence of dogs needing their anal 'glands' squeezed out at regular intervals. These glands are actually little sacs, just at the edge of the anus opening and contain a strong-smelling greasy substance used to 'mark' the freshly passed faeces for other animals to recognise. Over-production of the fluid causes the dog discomfort, and, when a suitable floor surface is available, the dog will 'scoot' along, leaving a trail of odorous matter. Occasionally, infection of the gland will alter the smell and this may result in other dogs being attracted to a female type odour. A course of antibiotics can directly solve this apparent behaviour problem.

Allergies can be detected by using a process of elimination in the diet.

Abscesses of the anal sacs are very painful and may require drainage, although they often swell and burst on their own with a sudden blood-stained discharge; flushing out and antibiotics may be required as treatment. Other glands around the anus may become cancerous, and attention is drawn to these if bleeding occurs. Adenomata are tumours found in the older male dog and require veterinary attention before bleeding occurs.

ARTHRITIS

This joint disease may be the result of an infection such as Lyme disease, but in many Boxers the condition is usually either due to joint wear and tear (degenerative) or as a result of an immune system reaction, such as rheumatoid arthritis or idiopathic arthritis. At first, degenerative arthritis improves with exercise, but as the disease progresses the dog will stiffen and on bending the joint often a painful, grating 'crepitus' can be found. Treatment will be aimed at keeping the dog mobile, excess weight should be lost and anti-inflammatory medication administered on a daily basis will relieve pain and discomfort. Blood tests and X-rays may be needed for investigating the extent of the arthritis. Some owners have had good results using supplements such as glycosaminoglycans. For the Boxer's comfort, provide soft, comfortable bedding and encourage short, frequent walks.

ATOPY

Sometimes known as the inhalant allergy, it is associated with many chronic skin diseases characterised by pruritus – a sensation within the skin that provokes the Boxer to scratch, lick, chew or rub himself to alleviate the irritation. It is not as common in Boxers as in some other breeds, but it may require specific tests and medication to relieve the itching. The signs do not usually develop until one to three years; roughened itchy, oozing skin may be caused by immune reactions to various allergens, such as fleas or pollen. There is an indication of an inherited tendency, and there is often a seasonal change if specific pollens are the cause. Seborrhoea may be found as a greasy or excessive scaly skin in some Boxers and is thought to be partially inherited and partially allergy induced.

BURNS & SCALDS

First-aid measures advise immediate cooling of the skin, by pouring cold water over the burn, repeatedly, for at least 10 minutes. Some scalds, after hot water or oil have been spilt, penetrate the coat and may not be recognised until a large area of skin and hair peels away, where the heat has killed the surface skin cells. As these injuries are considered to be very painful, analgesics (pain relief) should be obtained, and in anything but the smallest injured area, antibiotics would be advised, as secondary bacteria will multiply on exposed raw surfaces. Bandages and dressings are not a great help, but clingfilm has been used in some instances. Clipping the hair away over a large area surrounding the burn, then flushing the areas with saline, may be tolerated by the dog. An Elizabethan collar may be used to prevent the Boxer licking the area.

Exercise should be limited while a puppy is growing to prevent injury to joints that could later develop into arthritis.

In cases where the dog is showing signs of shock, intravenous fluid therapy may be a necessity.

CALCULI (BLADDER STONES)

Stones were often thought to be the cause of straining to pass urine and where these signs are shown a veterinary examination for bladder inflammation (cystitis) or tumours is advised. Calculi are deposits of mineral salts from the urine, either in the neck of the bladder or nearer the base of the penis in the male. Stones can also form in the kidneys and these cause the dog pain as they enter the ureters; the bladder is not affected at first.

Calculi are recognisable on X-ray or with ultrasound examinations. The obstruction may be partial when the dog or

bitch spends an unusually long time passing urine, or, more often in males, where no urine can be voided, the dog strains looking uncomfortable or in pain. An operation is usually necessary to remove calculi and diet advice will be given on how to avoid further attacks. Increasing the dog's water intake and providing opportunities for frequent bladder emptying are equally important in prevention.

CANCER – CARCINOMA

Cancer is slightly more prevalent in Boxers than in other breeds, but as all dogs are now living longer, it may seem that more dogs are affected by tumours, often in old age. One in every four dogs will be likely to suffer from one of the many types of cancer, but studies in the genetic make-up (genome) of the breed may well help to understand why some dogs are more prone to cancer than others. The genetic make-up of the breed was sequenced in 2004 and many benefits are expected in cancer control, both for dogs and for humans.

CONSTIPATION

Unless the Boxer is known to have consumed large quantities of bone or fibrous matter, straining may well be due to an enlarged prostate gland in the male, or a foreign body in the rectum. Increasing the dog's fluid intake and administering liquid paraffin is advised, but if the problem persists, the vet should be consulted.

CYSTITIS

Inflammation of the bladder is more common in the bitch and may be first noticed when the dog strains frequently, with only small quantities of urine passed each time. Bladder calculi are fairly common in both sexes and will cause cystitis, but bacteria reaching the bladder from outside the body is usually the cause. In all cases, the fluid intake should be reviewed, since a good 'wash through' of the bladder will reduce the risk of bacteria and mineral particles irritating the bladder lining. Medication with antispasmodics and an appropriate antibiotic will be required.

DIABETES

The Boxer has the best, inherited protection against diabetes mellitus than any other known breed. One of the two types of diabetes found in dogs, the 'sugar diabetes' known as DM, is seen most frequently in the older bitch. Caused by a lack of insulin to regulate the level of glucose in the blood, the signs of increased thirst, passing large quantities of urine, eye cataracts and muscle weakness are also associated with increased appetite and weight loss, as the dog attempts to satisfy the variations of his sugar levels. Diagnosis by urine and blood samples is followed by an injection of a suitable insulin subcutaneously once or more daily. Some types of endocrine disease, such as diabetes, may arise as a result of an immune-mediated

The Boxer has the best inherited protection against diabetes.

destruction of glandular tissues. Diabetes insipidus is less common in dogs and is related to the water control mechanism of the kidneys.

EYE PROBLEMS: CONJUNCTIVITIS, ULCERS

Conjunctivitis occurs in Boxers if the eye surfaces are exposed to dust or other irritants. Prominent eyes are more likely to suffer; the signs of a red eye, with a watery or crusty discharge, are easy to recognise. Chemicals and allergies cause irritation, but a presentation of acute, severe conjunctivitis may indicate the presence of a foreign body, such as a grass seed under the eyelids. Careful examination of the inner surfaces of both eyelids and the third eyelid is necessary to identify and remove foreign material.

Corneal erosion or 'Boxer

ulcers' is a particular problem, seen first as an excess watering and the screwing of the eyes against the light. This is due to the pain caused by the eye surface being pitted with exposed nerve endings. Specific veterinary treatment should be given as soon as possible (See inherited disorders, page 144).

EPILEPSY AND FITS

Seizures occur relatively commonly in dogs and represent an acute, and usually brief, disturbance of normal electrical activity in the brain, which can be distressing for both the patient and the owner. Most fits last only a short time (less than two minutes) and owners will often telephone for veterinary advice once the seizure is over. It is always best to have your dog examined afterwards by a veterinary surgeon, as soon as is practical, even if the seizure has stopped. Some fits are prolonged or very frequent, and these types of seizures may cause permanent brain damage. Once the fits have passed off, the dog may seem dull or confused for several hours. Medication, prescribed by the vet, can be used to control fits, but long-term treatment may be needed.

FRACTURES

Most broken bones are the result of an avoidable injury; an old dog with kidney disease may have brittle bones, but spontaneous fractures are quite rare even then. The treatment of a fracture will require the attention of your vet; there is little point in attempting first aid, as the Boxer will be in pain and will adopt the most comfortable position he can find. Natural pain killers, known as endorphins, kick in immediately, following such an injury. If there is a skin wound associated with the fracture, it should be covered to reduce bacterial contamination, reducing the risk of osteomyelitis, before the break in the bone can be satisfactorily repaired. X-rays will be necessary to confirm a crack or a major displacement of bones.

GASTRIC TORSION (BLOAT)

In the bloated stomach, gas and/or food stretches the stomach

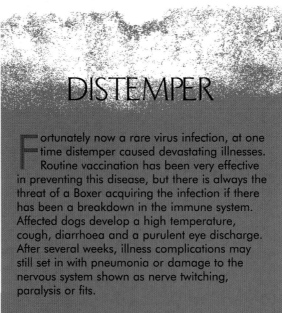

DISTEMPER

Fortunately now a rare virus infection, at one time distemper caused devastating illnesses. Routine vaccination has been very effective in preventing this disease, but there is always the threat of a Boxer acquiring the infection if there has been a breakdown in the immune system. Affected dogs develop a high temperature, cough, diarrhoea and a purulent eye discharge. After several weeks, illness complications may still set in with pneumonia or damage to the nervous system shown as nerve twitching, paralysis or fits.

many times its normal size, causing tremendous abdominal pain. For reasons we do not fully understand, the grossly distended stomach has a tendency to rotate, twisting off not only its own blood supply but the only exit routes for the gas inside. This condition is extremely painful and it is also rapidly life-threatening. A dog with a bloated, twisted stomach will die in pain in a matter of hours unless drastic steps are taken.

Classically, this condition affects dog breeds that are said to be 'deep chested,' meaning the length of their chest from backbone to sternum is relatively long while the chest width from right to left is narrow. This illness often occurs when the dog has eaten a large meal and exercised heavily shortly

afterwards. It is difficult to know why a particular dog bloats on an individual basis. No specific diet or dietary ingredient has been proven to be associated with bloat. Some factors found to increase the risk of bloat are feeding only one meal a day; having closely related family members with a history of bloat; eating rapidly; being thin or underweight; fearful or anxious temperament; and having a history of aggression towards people or other dogs. Male dogs are more likely to bloat than females and older dogs (7-12 years) are thought to be the highest risk group.

Factors decreasing the risk of bloat are possibly inclusion of table scraps in the diet; happy or easy-going temperament; eating 2 or more meals per day; soaking the biscuit for the meal.

The Boxer suffering this condition may have an obviously distended stomach especially near the ribs but this is not always evident depending on the dog's body configuration. The stomach area may feel quite rigid and the dog will retch but little is brought up. The dog will whimper and be quite obviously in pain. If this is seen, rush your dog to the vet immediately. The stomach needs to be untwisted and the gas released to save the dog and rapid iv fluids must be given to reverse the shock. The dog in most cases will have to undergo surgery, to allow the stomach to be tacked into normal position so that it may never again twist. Without this, the recurrence rate of bloat may be as high as 75 per cent! Assessment of the internal damage is also very important to recovery. If there is a section of dying tissue on the stomach wall, this must be discovered and removed or the dog will die despite the heroics described above. Also, the spleen, which is located adjacent to the stomach, may twist with the stomach. The spleen may require removal, too.

GASTRO-ENTERITIS
Vomiting, which is relatively common in dogs, can be a protective mechanism to try to prevent poisonous substances entering the body. Gastro-enteritis includes diarrhoea attacks, which act as a similar process to vomiting, by getting rid of undesirable intestine contents by washing them out. The production of extra mucus and intestinal fluid is seen with a rapid bowel evacuation movement. Both products of gastro-enteritis are objectionable – distressing to the dog and unpleasant for the owner, who may have to clean up afterwards. There are many causes, ranging

A sudden change of diet can cause a stomach upset.

from the simplest (such as the dog needing worming), to the complex interaction of viruses and bacteria that can cause an infection to spread through a kennel of dogs.

Dietary diarrhoea can occur after any sudden change in diet, such as scavenging (if a packet of butter is stolen, for example), or an allergy to a particular food substance or additive. If the signs of gastro-enteritis last more than 48 hours, a vet should be prepared to take samples and carry out other tests to look for diseases (such as pancreatitis, colitis or tumours), as some disorders may be life threatening. Treatment at home may be tried, using the principle of 'bowel rest', where the owner stops feeding for 48 to 72 hours; fluids are allowed, in repeated small

quantities. Ice cubes in place of water in the bowl may help to reduce vomiting. Electrolyte solutions, as used in 'Traveller's Diarrhoea', will help with rehydration. Once symptoms are alleviated, small feeds of bland foods, such as steamed fish or chicken, with boiled rice, may be gradually introduced. Where there is continual diarrhoea for three to four weeks, the disease is unlikely to resolve without identifying a specific cause and using appropriate treatment. The daily injection of maropitant may be prescribed by the vet, for the treatment of vomiting in combination with these supportive measures.

HEART AND CARDIAC DISORDERS
Heart disease may show itself in many forms. Young puppies may have abnormal heart sounds and have a congenital heart defect, but cardiac problems are most common in the slightly older Boxer. Reduced exercise and weight increase in the older dog are contributory factors to a failing heart. Medication has improved tremendously in recent years and can give a good long term prognosis. There are many disorders of the heart valves and blood vessels which can weaken the heart muscle, and a condition known as myocardial degeneration will often develop.

Dilated cardiac myopathy (DCM) is a heart disease found in Boxers, which are classed as a high risk breed, with up to 25% of dogs possibly at risk. Prompt diagnosis by the vet is important, since many dogs die within a year despite treatment. Syncope is the condition reached when the dog collapses; emergency treatment with oxygen and crate rest will be accompanied by appropriate heart medication. The UK Boxer Breed Council have a health committee which is working hard to find ways to prevent the spread of cardiomyopathy and has also been running seminars across the UK to educate people about the symptoms and forms this disease can take, as well as recommendations to breed away from lines which may be thought to be carrying a gene that can cause the disease.

Aortic Stenosis is one of the most common heart defects occurring in Boxers. Stenosis is a narrowing of the aorta, right below the aortic valve, which forces the heart to work harder to supply blood. Heart murmurs have been found to be common among boxers. It should be emphasised that these do not affect health in the great majority (95%) of dogs. Reduced blood flow can result in fainting and even sudden death. The disease is inherited but its mode of transmission is not known at this time. Diagnosis must be made by a veterinary cardiologist, after detection of a heart murmur.

Aortic stenosis is the heart condition most commonly associated with these heart murmurs, but cases of pulmonic stenosis and cardiomyopathy, as found in other breeds, have also been detected. Typically, clinical signs of aortic stenosis first appear in the young adult although,

If you have any concerns about your Boxer's health, do not delay in seeking veterinary advice.

rarely, puppies can be affected.

It should be stressed that minor "flow" murmurs are commonly found in young Boxer puppies, as in other breeds, but most disappear by about 16 weeks of age. Even if they persist there may be no cause for alarm if they are quiet. Such genuine "flow" murmurs" are not associated with heart disease in the adult. The incidence of Boxers with severe aortic stenosis has increased in recent years, although the number of cases is still very low in relation to the number of dogs bred.

To rectify the situation the UK Boxer Breed Council has, with the aid of veterinary cardiologists throughout the country, developed a system of testing based on simple stethescopic examination by the cardiologists. A breeding control scheme has also been established. A veterinary certificate of heart testing is provided to the owner with a copy for the animal's usual veterinary surgeon. Owners and breeders can make the appointment for heart testing from the age of twelve months onwards and this can be done either through their usual veterinary surgeon or sessions are often run at Dog Shows by the Boxer Breed Clubs, such as the British Boxer Club and various others across the country. Details of availability and dates of shows can be found by contacting the local breed club secretaries.

Therefore, should a heart murmur, or any heart condition other than a genuine puppy "flow" murmur, be recognised in a Boxer it should be referred to one of the cardiologists. The breeder and the Breed Council geneticist should be informed of the result. Dependant upon the findings the condition may be treatable.

If a puppy "flow" murmur is loud and persists, the vet in charge may recommend that further advice be sought from a specialist cardiologist.

Dogs and bitches used for breeding should all be properly tested for this disease and affected dogs will not be used in the breeding programme of reputable breeders. Those buying puppies should always ask if the parents have been heart tested.

HEPATITIS

Inflammation of the liver may be due to a virus, but it is uncommon in dogs that have been protected with vaccines, which also prevent the bacteria leptospira damaging the liver. Chronic liver disease may be due to heart failure, tumours or some type of toxicity; dietary treatment may help if there are no specific medicines to treat it. The skin condition known as hepato-

KENNEL COUGH

The signs of a goose-honking cough, hacking or retching that lasts from a few days to several weeks is due to damage at the base of the windpipe and bronchial tubes. The dry and unproductive cough is caused by a combination of viruses, bacteria and mycoplasma. Vaccination is helpful in preventing the disease, but may not give full protection, as strains of kennel cough seem to vary. The disease is highly contagious and is spread by droplets, so it may be acquired at dog shows or boarding kennels. An incubation period of five to seven days is usual. Veterinary treatment will alleviate the cough and reduce the duration of the illness.

cutaneous syndrome may affect the feet with non-healing sores.

HEARTWORM DISEASE

Heartworms are still uncommon in the UK, (although it is believed there may have been an outbreak in the New Forest), but are a major problem in the USA where they are spread by mosquitoes. Dogs can be protected from six to eight weeks of age with a monthly dose of the medication advised by the vet. A blood test can be taken to see if the heartworm antigen is present before commencing treatment, which can be repeated annually. The filarial worms live in the heart and blood vessels of the lungs and cause signs such as tiring, intolerance of exercise and a soft, deep cough.

INTERVERTEBRAL DISC DISEASE & PARALYSIS

The collapse or sudden weakness of the hindquarters may be due to pressure on the nerves of the spine that supply the muscles and other sensory receptors. The 'slipped disc', as it is commonly known, may be responsible, but any injury to the spine, a fibro-cartilage embolism, a fracture or a tumour may cause similar paralysis. The signs are similar with the dog dragging of one or both hind legs, lack of tail use and often the loss of bladder and bowel control. X-rays, a neurological assessment and possibly an MRI scan will be needed to be certain of the cause. Some cases respond well to surgical correction, but others will receive medical treatment, which may be effective and is less costly. Home nursing by the owner should include: keeping the dog clean and groomed, help with bladder or bowel movements, and carrying out any physiotherapy advised by the veterinary surgeon. Sudden movements in the case of spinal fractures must be avoided, as when carrying a patient with any back injury.

LEPTOSPIROSIS

Dogs that live in the country or swim in water may be more prone to this infection. Leptospira bacteria carried by rats can be found in pools and ditches where rodents may have visited. Annual vaccination against the two types of leptospira is advised. Treatment in the early stages using antibiotics is effective, but liver and kidney damage may permanently incapacitate the Boxer if the early signs, with a fever, are not recognised. Kidney and liver failure will lead to death. Treatment with antibiotics for two to three weeks will prevent the dog carrying leptospira and infecting others.

LYME DISEASE – BORRELIOSIS

This tickborne disease, affecting dogs, humans and, to a lesser extent, other domestic animals, is common in the USA. It is estimated that there may be a thousand cases a year in the UK. It is often seen as a sudden lameness, with a fever, or in the chronic form one or two joints are

The older Boxer is more likely to suffer from health problems.

affected with arthritis, often in the carpus (wrist joint), which alerts the Boxer owner to this disease. Exposure to ticks (Ixodes ricinus in Britain) should raise suspicions if similar signs develop, especially if a rash appears around the bite, which soon spreads. Treatment is effective and blood tests can be used to confirm Borrelia at the laboratory.

MANGE MITES

Several types affecting dogs are recognised and may be the cause of scratching, hair loss and ear disease. Sarcoptic mange causes the most irritation and is diagnosed by skin scrapings or blood tests. Demodectic mange is less of a problem and is diagnosed by skin scrapings or from plucked hairs. Otodectic mange occurs in the ears and the mite can be found in the wax. Cheyletiella is a surface mite of the coat; it causes white 'dandruff' signs and is diagnosed by coat brushing or sellotape impressions for microscope inspection. These mite infections first need identifying, but can then be treated by the vet with acaracide medication (such as amitraz, selamectin or imidacloprid and moxidectin). Previously, mange treatments usually required frequent bathing. The treatment will need to be repeated after 10 to 14 days to prevent reinfestation.

NEPHRITIS

Dogs may suffer acute kidney failure after poisoning, obstructions to the bladder or

after shock with reduced blood supply. Chronic nephritis is more common in older dogs, where the blood accumulates waste products that the damaged kidneys cannot remove. The nephritic syndrome is caused by an immune-mediated damage within the kidney. The signs of increased thirst, loss of appetite and progressive weight loss are commonly seen in kidney disease. Treatment of chronic renal failure is not reversible, but it aims to reduce the load on the remaining filter units (nephrons) and preventing further damage. Fluid intake should be encouraged if the dog is vomiting; intravenous drips will be needed to provide the liquid to help the kidney work. Taking the dog outside frequently to encourage bladder emptying also helpful. A special diet can also be beneficial; your vet can advise you as well as taking repeat blood samples to monitor the kidneys' workload. If the ill Boxer does not eat, he will start drawing on his own body protein and the condition known as azotaemia will result, with severe consequences.

A diet of high biological value protein, low in phosphate but rich in vitamin B, will be advised. Diuretics, to produce more urine, may be used in the nephritic syndrome cases.

OTITIS EXTERNA

Ear disease is less common in the Boxer than in dogs that have hanging-down ear flaps. When otitis occurs, a strong-smelling discharge develops and the dog shakes his head or may show a head tilt. Repeated scratching and head shaking may cause a blood haematoma, as a swelling underneath the skin of the ear flap. The presence of a grass seed in the ear canal is always a possibility in Boxers that have been out in long grass in the summer months. After becoming trapped by the hair, the seed can quickly work its way down the ear canal and can even penetrate the ear drum. The spikes of the grass seed prevent it being shaken out of the ear, and veterinary extraction of the seed is essential.

PARVOVIRUS

This virus, which infects younger dogs, is most dangerous to the recently weaned puppy. Vaccination schedules are devised to protect susceptible dogs; and the vet should be asked as to when, and how often, a parvo vaccine should be used in your locality. The virus has an incubation of about three to five days and attacks the bowels with a sudden onset of vomiting and diarrhoea. Blood may be passed, dehydration sets in and sudden death is possible. Isolation from other puppies is essential and the replacement of the fluids and electrolytes lost is urgent. Medication to stop the vomiting, antibiotics against secondary bacteria, and later, a smooth, bland diet, should be provided.

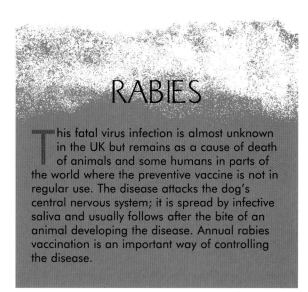

RABIES

This fatal virus infection is almost unknown in the UK but remains as a cause of death of animals and some humans in parts of the world where the preventive vaccine is not in regular use. The disease attacks the dog's central nervous system; it is spread by infective saliva and usually follows after the bite of an animal developing the disease. Annual rabies vaccination is an important way of controlling the disease.

PROSTATE DISEASE

Elderly Boxer males that have not been castrated may show signs of straining, which is often thought to be a sign of constipation, but an enlarged prostate gland at the neck of the bladder can be the real cause. Most often, it is a benign enlargement that causes pressure in the rectum, rather than blocking the bladder exit. Once diagnosed, hormone injections combined with a laxative diet are very effective.

PYODERMA

This is a term used by some vets for a bacterial skin infection; it is a condition seen in Boxers and is often associated with wet, oozing skin, known as 'wet eczema'. Treatment, such as an appropriate antibiotic, should be given to prevent licking and scratching, and clipping away the hair

encourages a dry surface where bacteria cannot multiply so readily. If the bacteria tunnels inwards, this results in the more difficult to treat furunculosis skin disorder.

PYOMETRA

At one time this was the commonest cause of illness in middle-aged and elderly bitches. The disease of the uterus would be seen in both those bitches never bred from and those who had litters early in life. The cause is a hormone imbalance, leading to an acute illness if bacteria invade the organ. Known as 'open pyometra', when a blood-stained mucoid discharge is seen, often with excessive licking around the vulva, it has been confused with a bitch coming into heat unexpectedly. It can be more difficult to diagnose the cause of illness when there is no discharge present (known as 'closed pyometra'), and other ways of testing the dog for the uterus disorder may be employed by the vet. Although medical treatments are available, it is more usual to perform a hysterectomy, especially if the bitch has come to the end of her breeding career.

RINGWORM

Ringworm is a fungus disease of the skin. It has nothing to do with worms, but it acquired the name from the circular red marks on the skin, following infection. It may appear as bald, scaly patches and will spread to children or adults handling the dog unless precautions are taken. Treatment will vary depending on the extent of the problem.

VESTIBULAR DISEASE
Middle-aged to elderly Boxers may be subject to a condition of a head tilt, often with the eye-flicking movements known as nystagmus. At one time it was commonly diagnosed as a 'stroke', because of its suddenness; the dog may circle or fall on one side, rolling as he cannot balance himself. Vestibular disease develops suddenly, but unlike the equivalent human stroke, there is no sign of bleeding or of a vascular accident in the brain. Recovery is slow, as the brain regains its balance centre after one to three weeks. Treatment by the vet will assist a return to normal, although some dogs always carry their head with a tilt.

INHERITED DISORDERS
Genetic diseases are not a new problem, but with better veterinary diagnostic methods and the fact that dogs now live longer, it is more likely that degenerative diseases are occurring. Healthy parents should always be selected to breed from. Much research on the inheritance of disease has taken place and single gene disorders are now being

identified, but the multiple gene disorders, especially where there is a relationship with nutrition and the environment, will take much longer to study. Fortunately, the breed of dog sequenced was the Boxer, since it was one of the breeds with the least amount of variation in its genome and therefore likely to provide the most reliable reference genome sequence.

EYE CONDITIONS
Abnormalities of the eyelids may be seen in the young, growing Boxer. Where the edge of the eyelid rolls inwards, as in entropion, the lashes rub on the eyeball surface (the cornea), causing intense irritation and eye watering. Distchiasis and ectopic cilia are examples of several other eyelid problems of hereditary origins. Most diseases such as these are amenable to surgery.

Conditions that affect the inside of the eye are more serious and can lead to blindness; the retina is the most important site of disease in the eye. A group of inherited diseases known as progressive retinal atrophy (PRA) are of particular importance and are known to occur in certain families. The disorder of folding of the retina, known as retinal dysplasia (RD), is seen from time to time in Boxers; large areas of detachment of the retina will cause blindness.

Cataracts are also found in Boxers. A cataract is the opacification of the fibres or capsule of the lens of the eye, ultimately resulting in blindness.

It may be present from birth, but in the older dog it must be distinguished from ageing changes, which result in an apparent blue colour of the lens, but through which the animal can still see. They may be left untreated or they can be surgically removed by specialist ophthalmic surgeons.

HIP DYSPLASIA
As an inherited disease in many dogs, the breed average score for Boxers is at the level of many other larger breeds. The basis of the control scheme is an X-ray examination of the young adult Boxer in order to identify early signs of hip structure malformation. Radiographs are taken by your vet after the dog is 12 months old and the photo is submitted for independent 'scoring' under the BVA/Kennel Club scheme. Hip dysplasia disease is a malformation of both the femoral head and acetabulum 'cup' of the hip, which results in lameness, pain and eventual arthritic changes. Anyone buying a puppy should enquire about the hip scores of the parents before completing the purchase.

COMPLEMENTARY THERAPIES
There is a wide choice of treatments that can be given to dogs over and above the type of medical or surgical treatment that you might expect when attending a veterinary surgery. Some of these alternative treatments have proved to benefit dogs while others are better known for their

effect on humans, where the placebo effect of an additional therapy has a strong influence on the benefit received.

Physiotherapy is one of the longest-tested treatments used in injuries and after surgery on the limbs. Chartered physiotherapists and veterinary nurses who have studied the subject work under the direction of the vet and can advise or apply procedures that will help mobility and recovery. Massage, heat, exercise or electrical stimulation are used to relieve pain, regain movement and restore muscle strength.

Hydrotherapy is very popular, as many dogs enjoy swimming, and the use of water for the treatment of joint disease, injuries or for the maintenance of fitness and health is very effective.

Acupuncture has a long history of healing, derived from Chinese medicine, involving the insertion of fine needles into specific locations in the body, known as 'acupuncture points'. The placing of the needles to stimulate nervous tissue is based on human charts and very good

With good care and management, your Boxer should live a long, happy and healthy life.

results have been reported when veterinary acupuncturists have selected suitable cases to treat.

Reiki as a form of laying on of a skilled operator's hands can have beneficial results. It is as equally convincing as acupuncture, and does not involve the dog tolerating needles in its body, but there are few qualified veterinary operators.

Magnetic therapy is perhaps more questionable in observed results; it involves applying magnetic products to the dog, to relieve pain and increase mobility.

Aromatherapy also has a following; it involves the treatment of dogs with natural remedies, essential oils and plant extracts, traditionally found in the wild.

Phytotherapy or herbal medicine has proven benefits and there are an ever increasing number of veterinary surgeons skilled in selecting appropriate plant products. Natural remedies are attractive to many users and provide a good alternative to many conventional veterinary treatments. Herbal drugs have become increasingly popular and their use is widespread, but licensing regulations and studies on interactions between herbal products and other veterinary medicines are still incomplete. One treatment for kennel cough with liquorice, thyme and echinacea helped cure a dog in 24 hours without antibiotics.

As with all alternative therapies it is necessary to consult a person who has the experience and specialised knowledge. Your Boxer's vet should be informed of any treatments since there are contraindications between some veterinary medicines and other remedies. Acute and/or chronic liver damage can occur after ingestion of some Chinese herbs and care in the application of 'natural products' is advised.

THE CONTRIBUTORS

THE EDITOR: VIV J MATTHEWS (BRUBOR)

Viv and her husband Danny received their first male Boxer, Samantony Eye of the Tiger at Brubor (Bruno), as a present when they got married in 1989, and that was the start of their career in Boxers. They began showing with limited success, following on with showing Sontano Red of Brubor, half brother to Bruno, who achieved Reserve Best in Show at Evesham Open Show in 1991, with Bruno getting RBOB at the same show.

In 1992 Viv and Danny got their first bitch from the well-known Maranseen kennel and Amy – Maranseen Cricket Crumpet at Brubor – was their first Crufts qualifier. They had a bitch puppy from Amy – Brubor Heavens Inspiration – and Katie did very well at shows, both at Open and at Championship level. Unfortunately she died young and only had one litter so they had to start their line again. They bought in a bitch from Les Wearing (Miofrey), who Viv named Miofrey Shirley Valentine of Brubor. This bitch was to prove their most successful so far; she did lots of winning, gained her stud book number, and had two fourths at Crufts before a spectacular win in a class of 27 bitches at Crufts in 2003. They had a litter from Shirley, and her daughter, Brubor Ryans Daughter, produced a lovely bitch called Brubor Sex in the City, sired by Ch. Winuwuk Lust in the Dust. She was their first to gain a Junior Warrant and her stud book number at 18 months of age.

Viv started judging in 1994, and her first B list appointment to judge Boxers was at South Wales Championship Show (without CCs) in July 2006 where she was delighted that her Best of Breed was a Champion, Ch./Ir. Ch. Sandcliffe Snog in the Fog!

Viv is Treasurer for the British Boxer Club for the last six years and also for the Boxer Breed Council.
See Chapter Two: The First Boxers; Chapter Three: A Boxer for your Lifestyle, and Chapter Seven: The Perfect Boxer.

SUE DRINKWATER (SULEZ)

Sue was first introduced to Boxers when she exercised one for pocket money as a teenager. She fell in love with Carlo, and, when his family moved away, jumped at the chance of having him join her family. In 1970, Sue met and married Les, the other half of the Sulez partnership, and one of the first things they bought was a Boxer puppy of their own, who later became best friend and guardian to their two daughters who eventually came along. From that day to this, they have never been without a Boxer or two in their home!

Sue has bred several Champions including litter brothers Ch. Sulez Whatever You Say and Ch. Sulez Whatever You Want for Manic (Top Sire 1993, owned by Julie Cook), Ch. Sulez Labelled With Love, (Top Boxer 1997) Ch. Sulez Shockwave, Ch. Sulez Sonicboom, Ch. Sulez Shorenuff, and numerous RCC winners. She has also bought in and campaigned Ch. Faerdorn Whatever Next at Sulez and Ch. Faerdorn So Glad for Sulez to their titles. Sue's biggest winner to date is the UK Breed Record Holder, Champion Sulez Blackmagic with 54 CCs, 30 BOB, 27 RCCs, Top Boxer 2003/4/5, Best in Show LKA 2006, and Cotswold Boxer Club Dog of the Year 2007.

In 2003, Sue was awarded the British Boxer Club's 'Boscar' for "The person or kennel that provides the most support to newcomers".

Sue is a Championship show judge and first awarded Challenge Certificates at the Cotswold Boxer Club Championship Show in 1997. She judged bitches at the Midland Boxer Club's prestigious two-day Millenium show, where each exhibit was given an individual written and graded critique. She has since judged Boxers in Ireland, Sweden, Australia and New Zealand. She is Vice Chairman of the British Boxer Club and also officiates as the club's show manger.
See Chapter One: Getting to Know the Boxer; Chapter Four: The New Arrival.

LAURA CLARK (CLARKENWELLS)

Laura started with her first Boxer in 1997 (having been brought up with one at home) – she loved her – but there were many battles over training, especially ringcraft! After two years Laura bought two puppies to show; neither worked out very well so she bred her first litter. Over the years, she has campaigned three home-bred puppies to the Junior Warrant, which qualifies them for Crufts for life, and has recently made her four-year-old dog Ch. Clarkenwells Rogue Trader up to a Champion – a dream come true! Both this dog and his daughter (Clarkenwells Vogue Trader) qualified for the national Boxer puppy and dog of the year competition 2008.
See Chapter Five: The Best of Care.

JULIA BARNES

Julia has owned and trained a number of different dog breeds, and is a puppy socialiser for Dogs for the Disabled. A former journalist, she has written many books, including several on dog training and behaviour. Julia is indebted to Di Wild for her specialist knowledge on Boxers. Di has owned (or been owned!) by Boxers for 40 years and has had fun with them as pets as well as competing with them in obedience, working trials and agility. She currently serves as the Vice President of the British Boxer Club.
See Chapter Six: Training and Socialisation.

DICK LANE BScFRAgSFRCVS

Dick qualified from the Royal Veterinary College in 1953 and then spent most of his time in veterinary practice in Warwickshire. He had a particular interest in Assistance Dogs: working for the Guide Dogs for the Blind Association and more recently for Dogs for the Disabled as a founder Trustee. Dick has been awarded a Fellowship of the Royal College of Veterinary Surgeons and a Fellowship of the Royal Agricultural Societies. He has recently completed an Honours BSc in Applied Animal Behaviour and Training, awarded by the University of Hull.
See Chapter Eight: Happy and Healthy.

USEFUL ADDRESSES

KENNEL & BREED CLUBS

UK
The Kennel Club
1 Clarges Street, London, W1J 8AB
Tel: 0870 606 6750
Fax: 0207 518 1058
Web: www.the-kennel-club.org.uk

National and regional breed clubs
To obtain up-to-date contact details for the following, please contact the Kennel Club:
• Anglian Boxer Club
• British Boxer Club
• Broadland Boxer Club
• Cotswold Boxer Club
• Essex and Eastern Counties Boxer Club
• Irish Boxer Club
• London and Home Counties Boxer Club
• Mancunian Boxer Club
• Merseyside Boxer Club
• Midland Boxer Club
• Northern Boxer Club
• Scottish Boxer Club
• South Wales Boxer Club
• South Western Boxer Club
• Trent Boxer Club
• Tyne Wear & Tees Boxer Club
• Boxer Breed Council

USA
American Kennel Club (AKC)
5580 Centerview Drive,
Raleigh, NC 27606, USA.
Tel: 919 233 9767
Fax: 919 233 3627
Email: info@akc.org
Web: www.akc.org

United Kennel Club (UKC)
100 E Kilgore Rd, Kalamazoo,
MI 49002-5584, USA.
Tel: 269 343 9020
Fax: 269 343 7037
Web:www.ukcdogs.com/

American Boxer Club.
http://www.americanboxerclub.org/

For contact details of regional clubs, please contact the American Boxer Club.

AUSTRALIA
Australian National Kennel Council (ANKC)
The Australian National Kennel Council is the administrative body for pure breed canine affairs in Australia. It does not, however, deal directly with dog exhibitors, breeders or judges. For information pertaining to breeders, clubs or shows, please contact the relevant State or Territory Controlling Body.

Dogs Australian Capital Territory
PO Box 815, Dickson ACT 2602
Tel: (02) 6241 4404
Fax: (02) 6241 1129
Email: administrator@dogsact.org.au
Web: www.dogsact.org.au

Dogs New South Wales
PO Box 632, St Marys, NSW 1790
Tel: (02) 9834 3022 or 1300 728 022 (NSW Only)
Fax: (02) 9834 3872
Email: info@dogsnsw.org.au
Web: www.dogsnsw.org.au

Dogs Northern Territory
PO Box 37521, Winnellie NT 0821
Tel: (08) 8984 3570
Fax: (08) 8984 3409
Email: admin@dogsnt.com.au
Web: www.dogsnt.com.au

Dogs Queensland
PO Box 495, Fortitude Valley Qld 4006
Tel: (07) 3252 2661
Fax: (07) 3252 3864
Email: info@dogsqueensland.org.au
Web: www.dogsqueensland.org.au

Dogs South Australia
PO Box 844
Prospect East SA 5082
Tel: (08) 8349 4797
Fax: (08) 8262 5751
Email: info@dogssa.com.au
Web: www.dogssa.com.au

Tasmanian Canine Association Inc
The Rothman Building
PO Box 116
Glenorchy Tas 7010
Tel: (03) 6272 9443
Fax: (03) 6273 0844
Email: tca@iprimus.com.au
Web: www.tasdogs.com

Dogs Victoria
Locked Bag K9
Cranbourne VIC 3977
Tel: (03)9788 2500
Fax: (03) 9788 2599
Email: office@dogsvictoria.org.au
Web: www.dogsvictoria.org.au

Dogs Western Australia
PO Box 1404
Canning Vale WA 6970
Tel: (08) 9455 1188
Fax: (08) 9455 1190
Email: k9@dogswest.com
Web: www.dogswest.com

INTERNATIONAL
Fédération Cynologique Internationalé (FCI)/World Canine Organisation
Place Albert 1er, 13, B-6530 Thuin, Belgium.
Tel: +32 71 59.12.38
Fax: +32 71 59.22.29
Web: www.fci.be/

TRAINING AND BEHAVIOUR

UK
Association of Pet Dog Trainers
PO Box 17, Kempsford, GL7 4WZ
Telephone: 01285 810811
Email: APDToffice@aol.com
Web: http://www.apdt.co.uk

Association of Pet Behaviour Counsellors
PO BOX 46, Worcester, WR8 9YS
Telephone: 01386 751151
Fax: 01386 750743
Email: info@apbc.org.uk
Web: http://www.apbc.org.uk/

USA
Association of Pet Dog Trainers
101 North Main Street, Suite 610
Greenville, SC 29601, USA.
Tel: 1 800 738 3647
Email: information@apdt.com
Web: www.apdt.com/

American College of Veterinary Behaviorists
College of Veterinary Medicine, 4474 Tamu, Texas A&M University
College Station, Texas 77843-4474
Web: http://dacvb.org/

American Veterinary Society of Animal Behavior
Web: www.avsabonline.org/

AUSTRALIA
APDT Australia Inc
PO Box 3122, Bankstown Square, NSW 2200,
Email: secretary@apdt.com.au
Web: www.apdt.com.au

Canine Behaviour
For details of regional behvaiourists, contact the relevant State or Territory Controlling Body.

ACTIVITIES

UK
Agility Club
http://www.agilityclub.co.uk/

British Flyball Association
PO Box 990, Doncaster, DN1 9FY
Telephone: 01628 829623

Email: secretary@flyball.org.uk
Web: http://www.flyball.org.uk/

USA
North American Dog Agility Council
P.O. Box 1206, Colbert,
OK 74733, USA.
Web: www.nadac.com/

North American Flyball Association, Inc.
1333 West Devon Avenue, #512
Chicago, IL 60660
Tel/Fax: 800 318 6312
Email: flyball@flyball.org
Web: www.flyball.org/

AUSTRALIA
Agility Dog Association of Australia
ADAA Secretary, PO Box 2212,
Gailes, QLD 4300, Australia.
Tel: 0423 138 914
Email: admin@adaa.com.au
Web: www.adaa.com.au/

**NADAC Australia (North American Dog Agility
Council - Australian Division)**
12 Wellman Street, Box Hill South, Victoria 3128,
Australia.
Email: shirlene@nadacaustralia.com
Web: www.nadacaustralia.com/

Australian Flyball Association
PO Box 4179, Pitt Town, NSW 2756
Tel: 0407 337 939
Email: info@flyball.org.au
Web: www.flyball.org.au/

INTERNATIONAL

World Canine Freestyle Organisation
P.O. Box 350122, Brooklyn, NY 11235-2525, USA
Tel: (718) 332-8336
Fax: (718) 646-2686
Email: wcfodogs@aol.com
Web: www.worldcaninefreestyle.org

HEALTH

UK
Alternative Veterinary Medicine Centre
Chinham House, Stanford in the Vale,
Oxfordshire, SN7 8NQ
Tel: 01367 710324
Fax: 01367 718243
Web: www.alternativevet.org/

British Small Animal Veterinary Association
Woodrow House, 1 Telford Way,
Waterwells Business Park, Quedgeley,
Gloucestershire, GL2 2AB
Tel: 01452 726700
Fax: 01452 726701
Email: customerservices@bsava.com
Web: http://www.bsava.com/

Royal College of Veterinary Surgeons
Belgravia House, 62-64 Horseferry Road, London,
SW1P 2AF
Tel: 0207 222 2001
Email: admin@rcvs.org.uk
Web: www.rcvs.org.uk

USA
**American Holistic Veterinary Medical
Association**
2218 Old Emmorton Road
Bel Air, MD 21015
Tel: 410 569 0795
Email: office@ahvma.org
Web: www.ahvma.org/

American Veterinary Medical Association
1931 North Meacham Road, Suite 100,
Schaumburg, IL 60173-4360, USA.
Tel: 800 248 2862
Fax: 847 925 1329
Web: www.avma.org

American College of Veterinary Surgeons
19785 Crystal Rock Dr, Suite 305
Germantown, MD 20874, USA.
Tel: 301 916 0200
Fax: 301 916 2287
Email: acvs@acvs.org
Web: www.acvs.org/

AUSTRALIA
Australian Holistic Vets
Web: www.ahv.com.au/

Australian Small Animal Veterinary Association
40/6 Herbert Street, St Leonards, NSW 2065
Tel: 02 9431 5090
Fax: 02 9437 9068
Email: asava@ava.com.au
Web: www.asava.com.au

Australian Veterinary Association
Unit 40, 6 Herbert Street, St Leonards, NSW
2065, Australia.
Tel: 02 9431 5000
Fax: 02 9437 9068
Web: www.ava.com.au

Australian College Veterinary Scientists
Building 3, Garden City Office Park,
2404 Logan Road, Eight Mile Plains, Queensland
4113, Australia.
Tel: 07 3423 2016
Fax: 07 3423 2977
Email: admin@acvs.org.au
Web: http://acvsc.org.au

ASSISTANCE DOGS

UK
Canine Partners
Mill Lane, Heyshott, Midhurst, GU29 0ED
Tel: 08456 580480
Fax: 08456 580481
Web: www.caninepartners.co.uk

Dogs for the Disabled
The Frances Hay Centre, Blacklocks Hill,
Banbury, Oxon, OX17 2BS
Tel: 01295 252600
Web: www.dogsforthedisabled.org

Guide Dogs for the Blind Association
Burghfield Common, Reading, RG7 3YG
Tel: 01189 835555
Fax: 01189 835433
Web: www.guidedogs.org.uk/

Hearing Dogs for Deaf People
The Grange, Wycombe Road, Saunderton, Princes
Risborough, Bucks, HP27 9NS
Tel: 01844 348100
Fax: 01844 348101
Web: www.hearingdogs.org.uk

Pets as Therapy
14a High Street, Wendover, Aylesbury, Bucks.
HP22 6EA.
Tel: 01845 345445
Fax: 01845 550236
Web: http://www.petsastherapy.org/

Support Dogs
21 Jessops Riverside, Brightside Lane, Sheffield, S9
2RX
Tel: 01142 617800
Fax: 01142 617555
Email: supportdogs@btconnect.com
Web: www.support-dogs.org.uk

USA
Therapy Dogs International
88 Bartley Road, Flanders, NJ 07836,.
Tel: 973 252 9800
Fax: 973 252 7171
Web: www.tdi-dog.o

Therapy Dogs Inc.
P.O. Box 20227, Cheyenne, WY 82003.
Tel: 307 432 0272.
Fax: 307-638-2079
Web: www.therapydogs.com

Delta Society - Pet Partners
875 124th Ave NE, Suite 101 • Bellevue, WA
98005 USA.
Email: info@DeltaSociety.org
Web: www.deltasociety.org

Comfort Caring Canines
8135 Lare Street, Philadelphia, PA 19128.
Email: ccc@comfortcaringcanines.org
Web: www.comfortcaringcanines.org/

AUSTRALIA
AWARE Dogs Australia, Inc
PO Box 883, Kuranda, Queensland, 488..
Tel: 07 4093 8152
Web: www.awaredogs.org.au/

Delta Society — Therapy Dogs
Web: www.deltasociety.com.au